BUSINESS AND GENERAL REFERENCE BOOK SERIES FROM IDG

Resumes For Dummies ™

Quick Reference Card

For Special Delivery

✔ If you fax or e-mail your resume, follow up with a hard copy by postal mail — it's a reminder that you're interested.

✔ Hand deliver your resume whenever possible. It's an attention getter if you ask the receptionist to deliver it to the addressee right away while you stand there.

✔ Print inexpensive business cards to use in networking prior to sending a resume.

✔ Make sure the card contains who you are—*financial planner, marketing specialist, electrical engineer* — as well as name and contact information.

✔ Exchange business cards with potential players in your career area but first, as a reminder, include where you met on the back of yours — *Fund for Animals fundraiser.*

✔ Call within two days to say you'd like to send your resume. If no job opening is on the horizon, send your resume anyway and ask if the contact knows another person to call, using the contact's name as a door opener.

Your Brisk Resume Review

Find the full, industrial strength KickButt Resume Checklist in Chapter 21. As a quick check, ask yourself

✔ Have I selected the best format for my situation?

✔ Is my resume focused, with a theme backed up by examples of my qualifications?

✔ Does my resume illustrate to an employer the benefits of interviewing me — how I can handle the job, have positive work attitudes, get along well with others?

✔ Does my resume stress my accomplishments and skills?

✔ Is my resume inviting to read because of good layout, adequate white space, emphasis on key points, and professional word processing and laser printing?

✔ Is my writing style clear, action-oriented, and well-organized?

✔ Could my resume be shortened without loss?

✔ Does my resume contain negative information?

✔ Are all my claims believable, backed up by examples and measurable results?

Resume Rights

✔ Research, research, research — know what skills, education, and experience you need for the job.

✔ Include a Job Objective or Skills Summary targeted to the job you want.

✔ Use white paper, standard typefaces, and lots of white space to create a computer-friendly, scannable resume.

✔ Highlight achievements that relate to the position you seek.

✔ Use the correct name, title, and address of your resume recipient.

P9-DDR-903

. . . For Dummies: Bestselling Book Series for Beginners

BUSINESS AND GENERAL REFERENCE BOOK SERIES FROM IDG

Resumes For Dummies™

Quick Reference Card

KICKBUTT JOBHUNT ORGANIZER

GETTING READY

Write resumes & cover letters
Choose employer targets
Research employers
Scan recruitment ads
Mouse the Internet for job sites

GOING PLACES

Ace job interviews
Trade some skin at networking meetings
Visit libraries & career centers
Sleuth job fairs
Join job hunt support groups

TARGETING PEOPLE

Reach employers & recruiters
Contact your contacts
Network on the Internet
Call job services and hotlines
Kiss-up to references

FOLLOWING UP

Draft interview thank-you letters
Write networking contact letters
Follow up with employers
Work out, chill out, cheer up
Repeat above actions until employed

Ready! -- Do First ◆◆◆◆◆◆◆◆◆◆◆◆◆◆◆◆◆◆◆◆◆◆◆◆◆◆◆◆◆◆◆◆◆

Yesterday ❑ _____ ❑ _____
❑ _____ ❑ _____
❑ _____ ❑ _____
This Week ❑ _____ ❑ _____
❑ _____ ❑ _____

Aim! -- Grab the Phone, Surf the Net ◆◆◆◆◆◆◆◆◆◆◆◆◆◆◆◆◆◆◆◆◆◆◆

Yesterday ❑ _____ ❑ _____
❑ _____ ❑ _____
❑ _____ ❑ _____
This Week ❑ _____ ❑ _____
❑ _____ ❑ _____

Fire! -- Beat the Pavement ◆◆◆◆◆◆◆◆◆◆◆◆◆◆◆◆◆◆◆◆◆◆◆◆◆◆◆◆◆◆

Yesterday ❑ _____ ❑ _____
❑ _____ ❑ _____
❑ _____ ❑ _____
This Week ❑ _____ ❑ _____
❑ _____ ❑ _____

Sizzle! -- Keep It Hot ◆◆◆◆◆◆◆◆◆◆◆◆◆◆◆◆◆◆◆◆◆◆◆◆◆◆◆◆◆◆◆◆

Yesterday ❑ _____ ❑ _____
❑ _____ ❑ _____
❑ _____ ❑ _____
This Week ❑ _____ ❑ _____
❑ _____ ❑ _____

® 1996, Joyce Lain Kennedy

. . . For Dummies: Bestselling Book Series for Beginners

Praise, Praise, Praise for Joyce Lain Kennedy

"Books by Ms. Kennedy are what got me started along the path of careers in education. Another individual has been converted by your books."

> — Patty McLarty, Reader, Gary, Indiana

"Joyce Lain Kennedy's distinguished career in occupational information has placed her leaps and bounds ahead of the rest."

> — Bob Calvert, Publisher, *Career News*

"Joyce Lain Kennedy has led the way in showing how technology has contributed an entirely new dimension to the job search. Her thorough knowledge of the basics lays a solid foundation for any beginner."

> — David Rouse, *Booklist*

"Joyce's ability to translate computer jargon into English for the non-techie has helped me and my non-technical friends relate to that entirely new dimension."

> — Judith Carbone, Career Development Center, George Mason University

"Joyce Kennedy is at the top of her field."

> — John D. Erdlen, CEO, Strategic Outsourcing, Inc.

"Joyce Lain Kennedy's expansive knowledge of the job search arena enables her to reach both the novice and experienced job-seeker. Truly she is the dean of careers journalists."

> — Susan Estrada, CEO, Aldea Communications, Inc.

RESUMES FOR DUMMIES™

by Joyce Lain Kennedy

IDG BOOKS WORLDWIDE

IDG Books Worldwide, Inc.
An International Data Group Company

Foster City, CA ♦ Chicago, IL ♦ Indianapolis, IN ♦ Southlake, TX

Resumes For Dummies™

Published by
IDG Books Worldwide, Inc.
An International Data Group Company
919 E. Hillsdale Blvd.
Suite 400
Foster City, CA 94404
http://www.dummies.com

Library of Congress Catalog Card No.: 96-75767

ISBN: 0-56884-396-8

Printed in the United States of America

10 9 8 7 6 5 4 3 2

1B/QW/QZ/ZW/IN

Distributed in the United States by IDG Books Worldwide, Inc.

Distributed by Macmillan Canada for Canada; by Contemporanea de Ediciones for Venezuela; by Distribuidora Cuspide for Argentina; by CITEC for Brazil; by Ediciones ZETA S.C.R. Ltda. for Peru; by Editorial Limusa SA for Mexico; by Transworld Publishers Limited in the United Kingdom and Europe; by Academic Bookshop for Egypt; by Levant Distributors S.A.R.L. for Lebanon; by Al Jassim for Saudi Arabia; by Simron Pty. Ltd. for South Africa; by Pustak Mahal for India; by The Computer Bookshop for India; by Toppan Company Ltd. for Japan; by Addison Wesley Publishing Company for Korea; by Longman Singapore Publishers Ltd. for Singapore, Malaysia, Thailand, and Indonesia; by Unalis Corporation for Taiwan; by WS Computer Publishing Company, Inc. for the Philippines; by WoodsLane Pty. Ltd. for Australia; by WoodsLane Enterprises Ltd. for New Zealand. Authorized Sales Agent: Anthony Rudkin Associates for the Middle East and North Africa.

For general information on IDG Books Worldwide's books in the U.S., please call our Consumer Customer Service department at 800-762-2974. For reseller information, including discounts and premium sales, please call our Reseller Customer Service department at 800-434-3422.

For information on where to purchase IDG Books Worldwide's books outside the U.S., please contact our International Sales department at 415-655-3172 or fax 415-655-3295.

For information on foreign language translations, please contact our Foreign & Subsidiary Rights department at 415-655-3021 or fax 415-655-3281.

For sales inquiries and special prices for bulk quantities, please contact our Sales department at 415-655-3200 or write to the address above.

For information on using IDG Books Worldwide's books in the classroom or for ordering examination copies, please contact our Educational Sales department at 800-434-2086 or fax 817-251-8174.

For authorization to photocopy items for corporate, personal, or educational use, please contact Copyright Clearance Center, 222 Rosewood Drive, Danvers, MA 01923, or fax 508-750-4470.

is a trademark under exclusive license to IDG Books Worldwide, Inc., from International Data Group, Inc.

Joyce Lain Kennedy

Joyce Lain Kennedy is author of the *Los Angeles Times* Syndicate's column **CAREERS**, now in its 27th year and appearing in more than 100 newspapers.

Her twice weekly columns are carried in the *St. Louis Post-Dispatch, Los Angeles Times, Dallas Morning News, Seattle Times, Louisville Courier Journal, Tulsa World,* and more.

Recognized as America's favorite careers journalist, Kennedy has received more than three million reader letters. In her column, she has answered in excess of 3,900 queries from readers.

Kennedy's wise counsel about job and career development address universal problems experienced by most working people—problems ranging from dealing with demotion to celebrating or coping with defining career moments. First to report on many new technologies and trends, Kennedy advises job seekers to relearn many strategies and tactics to prosper in a distinctly new job market.

She is the author or senior author of seven books, including *Joyce Lain Kennedy's Career Book* (VGM Career Horizons), *Electronic Job Search Revolution, Electronic Resume Revolution,* and *Hook Up, Get Hired! The Internet Job Search Revolution* (the last three published by John Wiley). The last three books are ground-breaking works for the new technology bringing people and jobs together. Joyce's other books for Dummies Press include *Cover Letters For Dummies* and *Job Interviews For Dummies.*

Writing from Carlsbad, California, a San Diego suburb, the dean of career columnists is a graduate of Washington University in St. Louis. Her e-mail address: jlk@sunfeatures.com.

Welcome to the world of IDG Books Worldwide.

IDG Books Worldwide, Inc., is a subsidiary of International Data Group, the world's largest publisher of computer-related information and the leading global provider of information services on information technology. IDG was founded more than 25 years ago and now employs more than 8,500 people worldwide. IDG publishes more than 270 computer publications in over 75 countries (see listing below). More than 90 million people read one or more IDG publications each month.

Launched in 1990, IDG Books Worldwide is today the #1 publisher of best-selling computer books in the United States. We are proud to have received eight awards from the Computer Press Association in recognition of editorial excellence and three from *Computer Currents'* First Annual Readers' Choice Awards. Our best-selling *...For Dummies*® series has more than 25 million copies in print with translations in 30 languages. IDG Books Worldwide, through a joint venture with IDG's Hi-Tech Beijing, became the first U.S. publisher to publish a computer book in the People's Republic of China. In record time, IDG Books Worldwide has become the first choice for millions of readers around the world who want to learn how to better manage their businesses.

Our mission is simple: Every one of our books is designed to bring extra value and skill-building instructions to the reader. Our books are written by experts who understand and care about our readers. The knowledge base of our editorial staff comes from years of experience in publishing, education, and journalism — experience which we use to produce books for the '90s. In short, we care about books, so we attract the best people. We devote special attention to details such as audience, interior design, use of icons, and illustrations. And because we use an efficient process of authoring, editing, and desktop publishing our books electronically, we can spend more time ensuring superior content and spend less time on the technicalities of making books.

You can count on our commitment to deliver high-quality books at competitive prices on topics you want to read about. At IDG Books Worldwide, we continue in the IDG tradition of delivering quality for more than 25 years. You'll find no better book on a subject than one from IDG Books Worldwide.

John Kilcullen
President and CEO
IDG Books Worldwide, Inc.

Acknowledgments

To my wonderful staff and many friends and colleagues who helped put this book together, thanks for the memories. It was fun.

At Sun Features Incorporated

Charity De Oca, Managing Editor

Charity's clarity of mind and editorial skills put this book's resumes and content way out in front of a kicking foot. A tough critic, she says revision is good for the soul. Assisting Charity assisting me on this book:

David R. Dunmeyer, Technical Wizard

As a Massachusetts Institute of Technology student, Dave preserved our words for eternity. His expertise and publishing precision fortunately compensated for my non-techie brain.

Erin Barry, Editorial Associate

Erin pitched in with ideas and words, permitting us to escape hammering deadlines that threatened to pound this work through the floor.

Muriel Turner, Office Manager Extraordinaire

Muriel kicked butt in the sanity department as manuscripts spewed from my printer and telephones rang off the hook.

Aaron ("A.J.") Nielsenshultz, Editorial Associate

A.J., reading resumes by the mountain, helped me avoid being buried in an avalanche of paper.

Christopher D. Lee, Technical Associate

Chris, working with dignity and discipline, battled our computers. And won.

At Dummies Trade Press

For choosing my work: Two Dummies Grins to **Kathleen A. Welton,** Publisher; and **Sarah Kennedy,** Executive Editor.

For editing my work: Two Dummies Handshakes to **Kathleen M. Cox,** Project Editor; and **Diane L. Giangrossi,** Copy Editor.

For promoting my work: Two Dummies Thumbs Up to **Stacy S. Collins,** Brand Manager; and **Jamie Klobuchar,** Assistant Brand Manager.

At Large

Special thanks for sharing your expertise to

James M. Lemke, University of California, Los Angeles

and to:

Regina Aulisio, The Wave Management Group, inc., San Diego, California

Richard H. Beatty, Brandywine Consulting Group, author of *The Resume Kit,* Malvern, Pennsylvania

Dr. Phyllis Brust and **Julie Ambrose,** Muhlenberg College, Allentown, Pennsylvania

Sharon Canter, Manpower, Inc., Milwaukee, Wisconsin

Douglas F. Coull, Advanced Personnel Systems, Oceanside, California

Wendy S. Enelow, The Advantage, Inc., and co-author of *The Resume Explosion* (audiocassette), Lynchburg, Virginia

John D. Erdlen, Strategic Outsourcing Inc., a division of Romac International Inc., Wellesley, Massachusetts

Mark Gisleson, Gisleson Writing Services, Minneapolis, Minnesota

John Lucht, The Lucht Consultancy, and author of *Rites of Passage at $100,000+: The Insider's Lifetime Guide to Executive Job-Changing*, New York City

Louis Masterson, Louis Thomas Masterson & Company, Cleveland, Ohio

Patrick O'Leary, United Parcel Service Airlines, Louisville, Kentucky

Yana Parker, author of *Damn Good Resume Guide*, Oakland, California

Craig VonKouwenberg, The Shelbourne Group, Lancaster, Pennsylvania

Publisher's Acknowledgments

We're proud of this book; send us your comments about it by using the Reader Response Card at the back of the book or by e-mailing us at feedback/dummies@idgbooks.com. Some of the people who helped bring this book to market include:

Acquisitions, Development, & Editorial

Project Editor: Kathleen M. Cox

Executive Editor: Sarah Kennedy

Copy Editor: Diane L. Giangrossi

Technical Reviewer: James M. Lemke

Editorial Manager: Kristin A. Cocks

Editorial Assistants: Chris H. Collins, Kevin Spencer, Ann Miller

Special Help

Jeffrey R. Cox

Production

Project Coordinators: Valery Bourke, J. Tyler Connor

Layout and Graphics: Cameron Booker, Cheryl Denski, Angela F. Hunckler, Todd Klemme, Jane E. Martin, Anna Rohrer, Brent Savage, Gina Scott

Proofreaders: Kathleen Prata, Christine Meloy Beck, Michael Bolinger, Dwight Ramsey, Carl Saff, Robert Springer

Indexer: Anne Leach

General & Administrative

IDG Books Worldwide, Inc.: John Kilcullen, President & CEO; Steven Berkowitz, COO & Publisher

Dummies, Inc.: Milissa Koloski, Executive Vice President & Publisher

Dummies Technology Press & Dummies Editorial: Diane Graves Steele, Associate Publisher; Judith A. Taylor, Brand Manager

Dummies Trade Press: Kathleen A. Welton, Vice President & Publisher; Stacy S. Collins, Brand Manager

IDG Books Production for Dummies Press: Beth Jenkins, Production Director; Cindy L. Phipps, Supervisor of Project Coordination; Kathie S. Schutte, Supervisor of Page Layout; Shelley Lea, Supervisor of Graphics and Design

Dummies Packaging & Book Design: Kavish+Kavish, Cover Design

◆

The publisher would like to give special thanks to Patrick J. McGovern, without whom this book would not have been possible.

◆

Contents at a Glance

Cartoons at a Glance

By Rich Tennant
Fax: 508-546-7747
E-Mail: the5wave@tiac.net

Page 189

Page 111

Page 151

Page 9

Page 81

Table of Contents

Introduction

*T*o get a job in today's tough job market, you must start with a KickButt resume. Nothing less will do.

KickButt: A compound word coined from "kick butt." Admittedly, the term as applied to resumes comes from the humorist Dave Barry School of Logic. But does it communicate the unbeatable, persuasive punch that contemporary resumes must have? You bet your assets it does.

To be certain this book is lexicographically correct, my team and I cruised local malls, bingo halls, and mosh pits to conduct an author-on-the-street random sampling of ordinary mortals (and anyone else who didn't tell us to take a hike). We asked what they think the term *KickButt resume* means. Don't think about it for five years — just blurt it out, we said.

Among dozens of colorful replies — not all of which were fit to print — here are our five favorites:

A KickButt resume is

- A resume that doesn't get shoved around, but competes, compels, and conquers
- A pumped-up resume that doesn't take no for an answer
- The opposite of mealy-mouthed . . . an aggressive, pit-bull of a resume that shows who must be seen — who wins, who loses
- A Terminator resume that doesn't get trashed
- A tough-minded resume that pounds the table and says, "Hey, don't pass me over. Pay attention! I'm the *one* for this job!"

These solicited resume definitions suggest that people perceive a KickButt version as one hot honey of a sales tool. Just what you need!

A Time for KickButt Resumes

Be honest in answering this short quiz:

- ✔ Is your current self-marketing document getting so little attention that you suspect it has "IGNORE ME" scrawled in invisible ink?
- ✔ Is your resume so b-o-r-i-n-g that you nod off while updating it?
- ✔ Is your first instinct to give your resume the toe — if not a less-respectful digit?

If you answered "Yes" to any of these questions, change your resume! Today! Your resume holds your future in its inky little black lines, so isn't it time to zip it up with zest and pizzazz? This book shows you in detail how to add a flying kick of grabby substance and attention-riveting words. A KickButt resume gives you a much better chance to conquer a contemporary job market that's infinitely different and ever more volatile than it was in your parents' day — no matter how old you are.

Job market watch

To understand the forces at work in the job market today, it helps to review the dramatic changes that have taken place over the last 50 years. Once you can see and appreciate the scope and pace of the changes that have taken place, you can also see and appreciate why you need a KickButt resume to propel you ahead of the crowd.

The boom years

Looking back at the late 1940s through the 1960s — high times in the post World War II boom — thriving industries in developed nations created millions of good jobs, and most seekers could find livelihoods of their choosing.

By the 1970s, the bulk of the babies born in the boom years (the baby boomers) hit their 20s, flooding the labor market with young, college-educated workers — battalions of doctors, lawyers, and MBAs storming out of professional schools in record numbers, along with smart and savvy engineers, accountants, advertisers, and entrepreneurs.

Also in the 1970s, one of the century's most significant sociological trends took shape: Tens of millions of women — a veritable tidal wave — exchanged their aprons for paid work outside the home, significantly enlarging the work force and creating new pressures for good jobs.

The decline of heavy industry

In the United States, the growth of the service economy gained speed over traditional manufacturing jobs as the ranks of $25-an-hour industrial plant workers were drastically thinned by massive layoffs. So many plants were closed and jobs were lost that the industrial heartland states of Pennsylvania, Ohio, Michigan, and Illinois turned into the *rust belt* as once-prosperous cities rushed to cope with a declining tax base.

At the same time that good manufacturing jobs were disappearing, more good jobs were being created in the service and information technology sectors. Knowledge workers began to dot the marketplaces of the U.S. and other developed economies around the globe. The development of a digital economy, fueled by the rapid growth of computer technology, was under way.

By the 1980s, technology took hold with revolutionary vigor. Computers and other machines replaced traditionally skilled laborers as automation claimed thousands of jobs in a variety of industries. By mid-decade, the developed world began to fully recognize the employment challenges of the digital economy. New structures, new requirements, and new rules crowded into the employment marketplace.

The middle-class squeeze

More changes in the 1980s: a tilt toward a two-tiered society. At the top are perched the new high-paid knowledge workers; at the bottom rest the many low-paid manual laborers. The economic middle class began to thin out.

- In winner-take-all power plays, huge prizes went to money movers, such as merger lawyers and mortgage bankers, and smaller rewards reached product producers such as manufacturing engineers and scientists. Few rewards remained for the average worker.

- Service sectors with lower paying jobs grew dominant in industrialized nations.

- No longer could just any warm body stumble into employment: The idea that only serious scouting could find good jobs was ready for prime time.

- Companies discovered that slashing the number of employees and their healthcare and retirement benefits was an investor-friendly way of controlling upward-spiraling costs.

Investors in the 1980s and early 1990s favored merging companies, downsizing, restructuring, reengineering, reducing the work force, and exporting jobs. Payroll-cutters justified these actions as necessary for a competitive and healthy bottom line. But middle managers and secretaries, who have joined the plant workers in the unemployment lines, didn't buy the explanations offered by corporate CEOs, many of whom annually take home millions of dollars in pay and stock options as a reward for cutting jobs.

Corporate executives today have their strongest financial incentive ever to maximize every hire and minimize every expense. Between management and employees, distrust and disrespect have begun to replace loyalty and civility. The cozy dream of reliable, family-nurturing wages until death-do-we-part is fading fast. Job insecurity has become rampant. It's harder than ever to get a job and keep it, much less grow in it.

More massive changes ahead

In the late 1990s, we face even more startling and massive changes as the world's economies, technologies, and workers rewrite the notion of work itself. The project manager — brought into a company for a limited time to honcho a task with a beginning, a defined scope, and an end — is becoming a familiar face. The temporary or part-time worker who handles professional and managerial work is no longer a rarity.

In developed nations, people meeting for the first time often say, "What do you do?" In an age of ever-changing assignments many people are finding that question increasingly hard to answer.

Not only are people grasping at a series of time-limited jobs, but futurists proclaim that, for the first time, human labor is being written out of the of the production process. They speculate that the end is near for work that comes bundled in jobs. In the 21st century, the struggle for jobs will be over, futurists say and a new — not yet defined — concept of work will take over. We need to be ready for anything.

Whatever develops on tomorrow's job scene, a certainty exists today: At this very minute, most job seekers find themselves in fierce competition for good jobs with long-term promise. Until further notice, new graduates and veteran workers alike are of necessity evolving into a new species — a ravenous breed of self-contractors always on the prowl for more and better work.

It's the '90s, and the workin' ain't easy

From the trip down memory lane, discussed in the previous section, you can see us now in the most competitive employment times since the 1930s. You see that, in today's world, you perform or you perish. You make your numbers or you fall behind. You meet deadlines or you greet dead ends. Employment-for-life is outmoded; job-hopping, by choice or by chance, is the wave of the future. Many of you will consider yourselves lucky to find a job home that lasts at least five years before you decide to leave or your position ends.

To cope, you take a good, permanent, core job when you can find one. When you can't find what you want, you move your career onto a jungle gym, swinging from job to job, going wherever opportunity takes you. *Have skills, will travel*. Your resume is your passport. And this book will help put you on the map.

My team and I have worked overtime to bring you a book that captures the "todayness" of contemporary resume content, formatting, styles, and distribution methods. But it's up to you to craft a stellar portrait.

Put on a Happy Face

Although times have changed and resumes have changed, some things remain the same. And the most important of these unchanging truths is the critical necessity for you to have an upbeat attitude throughout your job search. This book takes a light and breezy tone for a reason. In the litany of life's twists and turns, losing a job is always a heartbreaker. Sometimes, it's downright grim. So is being young and unable to find an employer willing to take a chance on you.

- ✔ You may feel rejected or betrayed, depressed, useless, angry at the system, or too old to begin again.
- ✔ You may have followed all the "rules" — such as holding an advanced degree from a respected college, demonstrating solid analytical and communications skills, possessing computer literacy, and having a proven record of achievement and glowing references — and still be job shopping after a year of unemployment.
- ✔ You may worry about losing your home or your marriage.
- ✔ You may be full of doubt about whether you'll ever find work
- ✔ You may be frozen with fear of the future.

All these reactions are normal, possible, and to be expected. Unless you have enormous inner reserves and a direct line to your higher being, your self-esteem probably falls on the minus side during times of unemployment.

In your despair, you may not feel like smiling. Yet — like one of those really important things you learned in kindergarten — smile you must. Study after study shows that individuals of good cheer tend to work well with others — a critical employability skill in today's team-driven workplaces. And individuals with good cheer have the energy to pursue and sustain a competitive job search without cracking.

Smiles are the language of job finding.

People don't go out of their way to hire a person who is beaten down. Employers offer a hiring hand not because they feel sorry for you, but because they value your skills. In today's chancy world where employers roll the dice every time they open their doors, they prefer to hire can-do, supercharged, happy, upbeat people. Downers are out.

When your job search stalls, surround yourself with chipper, outgoing, joyful people. Find at least one reason each day to say "cheese." Job seekers whose spirits soar fare much better than those whose spirits drag on the ground. Put some wind under your wings.

What's in This Book

To give you an idea of what's ahead, here's a breakdown of the five parts in this book. Each part covers a general topic. The part's individual chapters dig into the details.

Part I: Selling Yourself as a Hot Hire

Part I shows you the basics of presenting yourself as a hot hire; it explains formats, contents, words, and appearance.

Part II: Creating Your KickButt Resume

Part II reveals the secrets of how to lay the personal groundwork that rocket-fuels a KickButt resume.

Part III: Solving Specific Resume Stumpers

Part III has all the best and latest solutions to specific problems in a resume, from ageism to disability to career-changing.

Part IV: Samples of KickButt Resumes

Part IV presents examples of KickButt resumes, arranged by career fields and problem types.

Part V: The Part of Tens

Part V, the Part of Tens, takes you on a tour of top-ten lists that serve as handy affirmations of key points to remember.

Icons Used in This Book

When something in here is particularly noteworthy, I go out of my way to make sure it stands out. That's what these neat icons are for. They mark text that (for one reason or another) you *really* need to pay attention to. Here's a quick scan of the ones awaiting you in this book and what they mean.

You'll see this symbol noting hard-charging, power tips to make your resume nearly invincible.

This icon highlights tips for the seasoned pro who's been around the business block, but whose experience may need a jump start.

This icon signals you to pay attention so that you don't come across as a clueless beginner, even if you are one.

This icon indicates advice from whizzes in the job-finding business.

This icon spotlights differences of opinion in the art of resume writing.

This icon zeroes in on a snack-sized bit of information to help you see your presentation through the resume reader's eyes.

This icon reminds you that technology is changing the world. You don't need to know this stuff, but it's a good idea to be in on it.

This icon shows when it's important for you to note words of wisdom.

The warning icon says it all: this information can stop you from making a job-killing mistake. Pay attention to these icons to keep your job search from abruptly ending.

This icon notes the fundamental facts of resume preparation and job hunting. When you need to get down to basics, this is it.

You will also notice text with lines above and below it. That's meant to signify resume excerpts.

When the Going Gets Tough, the Tough Go Writing

Whether you are a new graduate starting out — or a seasoned ace who's been aced out — this book shows you how to boot the competition with a block-buster resume that says you're a candidate too good to pass over.

Start writing. Start kicking some butt.

Part I
Selling Yourself as a Hot Hire

The 5th Wave   By Rich Tennant

"YOU MAY BE 'LORD OF THE JUNGLE' WHERE YOU COME FROM, PAL. BUT HERE YOU'RE JUST ANOTHER APPLICANT FOR THE SHIPPING DEPT."

In this part ...

Contents — that's the operative word for your KickButt resume—contents that say "Hire me fast!" This part shows you what to put in the resume and how to pull together its strands in a way that inspires managers to book face-time with you ASAP.

Chapter 1

What Your Resume Reveals about You

● ●

In This Chapter

▶ Meeting the KickButt resume—a new dimension in resumes

▶ Exploring electronic resumes

▶ Doing your homework to create KickButt resumes

▶ Deciding how many resumes you need

● ●

ou say you want a job that you don't have to save up for? You say you're tired of selling off a piece of your life in return for forgettable pay in going-nowhere jobs? Or you're fed up with starving as a student? You say you want a job that speaks fluent money with an interesting accent? Sounds good. But that's not *all* you want, you say?

You want a job that puts jingle in your pocket and paper in your bank account. Yes. But you also want *meaningful* work.

I understand. What you want is a job that you love to get up in the morning to do and that pays major money, has first-class benefits, provides self-actualizing challenge, doesn't disappear overnight, and maybe sends you off on pleasant travels periodically. In Hollywoodspeak, what you want is one of those above-the-line jobs that star you in Purposeful Endeavor.

Okay, you've got the right book.

Having tracked the jobmarket for a quarter of a century, I can assure you that, despite the corporate devastation scourging the developed nations of the world, millions of above-the-line jobs still exist. These jobs are going to people who, with KickButt resumes and stiff-butt discipline, have found out how to outrun the crowd.

Read this book's Introduction, if you haven't already. There, I document the forces of change that are overwhelming the business world. It's not your father's workforce anymore. Once you recognize this fact, you'll understand why you need to change your strategy to save yourself endless wheel spinning and heartburn if, heaven forbid, you're still job hunting in the past. This chapter tells why you need a KickButt approach to preparing your resume in order to make the new work place work for you.

What should you do when you want to change careers and you don't know exactly to what? Sorry, but you're not ready to write a KickButt resume. First clarify your direction, whether through introspection or professional employment help. When you've identified your new career, you can get tips for making a smooth transition in Chapter 12.

Really, Must You Have a Resume?

A resume used to be a simple, low-key sheet or two of paper outlining your experience and education, with a list of references at the end. That kind of resume is now a museum piece.

By contrast, your KickButt resume is a specially prepared *sales presentation*. Created as a marketing tool to persuade a potential employer that you are the best one to do the job you seek, your resume is a self-advertisement that showcases your skills. With a series of well-written statements that highlight your previous work experience, education, and other background information, your resume helps prove what you say about your achievements, accomplishments, and abilities. It tells an employer you have positive work attitudes and strong interpersonal skills.

As a sales presentation, your resume answers questions about you as a *product:*

- ✔ What skills do you bring to the organization?
- ✔ Why are you worth the money you hope to earn?
- ✔ How are you better than other candidates for the job?
- ✔ Can you solve company or industry problems?

In every statement, your resume strategically convinces employers that you can do the job, have positive work attitudes, and get along with others. Your resume — whether stored on paper or in the rapidly expanding electronic universe — helps employers see how they could benefit by interviewing you.

Periodically, job guide writers, with gunslinging self-assurance, assert that resumes are unnecessary baggage. These critics insist that the best way to find a job is to network and talk your way inside. Put wax in your ears on this one. The only people for whom the no-resume advice is okay are those who can leave talk-show hosts struggling to get a word in edgewise. Very few people are extroverted and glib enough to carry the entire weight of their employment marketing presentations without supporting materials.

More importantly, you need a resume because most employers say you need a resume. No one has spare minutes today. People are too busy to enjoy long lunch hours. Employers refuse to take oral histories when you call to "ask for a few minutes of time to discuss opportunities." Those days are gone.

Even if — as a corporate executive's child, pal, or hairdresser — you land on a payroll by fiat, somewhere along the way you'll need a resume. At some point, people who make hiring decisions insist on seeing a piece of paper or a computer screen that spells out your qualifications. Resumes are an important first step on the road to the perfect job.

Remember: Resumes open doors to job interviews; interviews open doors to jobs.

First impression: Lasting impact

What does your resume reveal about you? Right off the bat, your resume reveals whether you're willing to take the time to discover what a prospective employer wants done that you are well-qualified to do. It shows the health of your judgment and the depth of your commitment to work.

Whether you are an aspiring rookie, a veteran ace campaigner, or simply someone who seeks to leave miles of bad road to speed along the fast track to a super career, launch your resume-writing venture by putting yourself inside the employer's life form. The development of an inside perspective begins with both old- and new-fashioned research. Your overwhelming impulse may be to assume that you can write a resume out of your own head and history — that dogged, time-eating research makes a nice add-on, but is not essential. Don't listen. *At the core of a KickButt resume is research, research, and more research.*

Research into your prospective company — in this usage, *company* means nonprofit organizations and government agencies as well as private companies — lets you glimpse how you might fit into the company and what you can offer it. Research gives you a sound basis for selecting those areas to include in your resume that demonstrate good judgment and commitment.

When you know what an employer is willing to employ someone to do, you can tell the employer why you should be the one employed. *In a tight job race, the candidate who knows most about the employer has the edge.*

What's new in resumes

Attention! Atención! Achtung! Chui! Attenzione!

The big worldwide news in resumes is *technology.*

Technology expresses itself in two major ways:

- ✔ Resumes that are transmitted via fax, e-mail, and over the Internet — across town or across the globe
- ✔ Resumes that are scanned, read, screened, and electronically filed by job computers

Don't blink if you want to stay current with the employment technology that's sweeping the planet with lightning speed. Here are two quick examples: After only 18 months (mid-1994 to 1996), many thousands of companies have established an Internet presence with World Wide Web pages; in a similar time frame, the U.S. Department of Labor has geared up to pump more than *300,000 job openings a day* through the Web, a figure headed toward one million jobs a day within a few years. Developments like these are changing the face of job searching in America and around the world.

The rush of electronic employment automation goes way beyond the sheer joy of gadgeteering. The first trend, electronic distribution of resumes, is taking place for economic and time considerations — and because the technology is relatively cheap and available. The second trend, computer-friendly resumes, is spreading because companies are finding it too costly to sort through mounds of resumes by hand.

If you need to play catch-up on the newest wave of electronic job searching, a wide-ranging discussion of how-to-do-it processes in electronic jobmarket trends fill three other books that I've written[1]. The following sections cover a few highlights.

---

[1] A comprehensive discussion of computer-friendly and Internet-mailed resumes is available in *Electronic Resume Revolution* and *Electronic Job Search Revolution,* both books by Joyce Lain Kennedy and Thomas J. Morrow. Also see *Hook Up, Get Hired! The Internet Job Search Revolution,* by Joyce Lain Kennedy. (All books published by John Wiley & Sons, Inc.)

E-mail and Internet transmission

It's in your best interests to get an e-mail (electronic mail) address to benefit from low-cost communications virtually anywhere in the world. (Yes, just as when making rabbit stew you must first catch a rabbit, in making your e-mail address arrangements, you must first catch a computer.)

E-mail lets you communicate across any number of miles without paying long-distance telephone charges. You can job prospect and network for pennies. For less than $10 a month, you can hook up to e-mail and the Internet through one of the commercial online services such as America Online, CompuServe, and Prodigy. Toll-free directory information (800-555-1212) provides their toll-free telephone numbers for details.

Along with letting you enjoy champagne communications on a beer budget, an e-mail address helps employers see that you're ready to take on the challenges of the 21st century. No hedgehog stick-in-the-mud, you! Besides, an e-mail address following your telephone number just looks cool — especially if you're on the shady side of 50 and could use a huge image rehab.

When you don't know how to get yourself an e-mail address, ask for consumer guidance from a cyberlibrarian (a librarian who specializes in computerized information retrieval) or a salesperson at a computer store. Add the e-mail address to your paper resume, along with the traditional contact information of address and telephone number.

A personal World Wide Web page on the Internet is a related and significant development, to date used chiefly by technical and creative people. An interactive, text-based personal Web page is actually not one but a number of pages supercharged with graphics — and perhaps with sound and video — serving as a kind of electronic modeling clay. Are you a software engineer? Show your programming genius. Architect? Flash your building designs. Writer? Light up the screen with excerpts from a magazine article, book chapter, or school essay.

If you are the beneficiary of thimbleful of magic technical genes (or have a friend who is) or if you are willing to pay a professional Web page designer, look into launching your own Web page resume. You can also get a copy of *Creating Web Pages For Dummies* to help in your efforts. But a word of warning: A weak personal Web page is a monument to limp design skills or, worse, to poor judgment. Better not to post a Web page than to post it badly. See Chapter 2 for some tips on setting up a Web page.

Scannable resumes

Electronic applicant tracking, used by growing numbers of businesses and organizations, uses digital imaging technology that keeps your resume active for years in a computer system.

After the resumes are scanned into a computer database, employers with a job to fill can search the database's resumes by *keywords* (I call them KeyWords) that define such things as your work history, years of experience, education, and skills. When your skills match the computer's search instructions, your resume is summoned to the company's employment screen and, from there, rocketed to the appropriate hiring managers. If the managers like what they see, they'll get in touch with you by telephone, postal mail, or e-mail. I talk more about KeyWords in Chapter 4.

Don't let the prospect of computer "control" scare you. The computer search makes the first cut, the screening, but people still make the selection.

Many companies solicit resumes over the Internet, giving you instructions online about how to submit your resume, whether by e-mail, the Internet, or fax.

Note one big change: Job computers usually prefer nouns (designer, marketing research, benefits analysis) over verbs (designed, market researched, analyzed). Using nouns as KeyWords in your resume is the smart way to make sure your resume gets the broadest possible coverage.

CVs and portfolios

Other formats and styles also appear on the scene. Some of these are unfamiliar in the United States, such as the international *curriculum vitae* ("CV" for short) used in Europe and Asia. The CV crosses borders to perform far more comprehensively (and intrusively) than the overview resume favored in the United States. In the CV format, you let everything hang out but your mother's maiden name, while in a U.S.-style resume, you rock 'em and sock 'em with reasons to call you for a job date.

Another fairly new format is the *portfolio* resume, which includes work samples, much like the portfolio of an artist or advertising copywriter. The portfolio has turned up in the 1990s because mushrooming numbers of independent contractors and temporary workers believe work samples are one way to prove their ability to adapt quickly to different environments. Even if you don't plan to present a portfolio right now, a career-focused collection of your visual information is an interesting idea for self-clarification and helps you prepare for unexpected requests from employers. I talk more about these "paper" resume formats in Part II.

When You Need More than One Resume

When do you need more than one version of your resume? Most of the time. Following the usual approach, you develop a core resume and then amend and slant it to fit specific positions, career fields, or industries.

The ultimate KickButt resume, like a custom-made suit, is tailored to the job that you want. After researching the target company and position, you can make your resume fit the job description as closely as your work and education history allows.

What research do you need?

- ✔ At minimum, you should know the scope of the position and the skills that the company is looking for.

- ✔ For a more comprehensive approach, learn the company's history, growth and acquisition record, products and services, how recently and deeply it has downsized personnel, corporate philosophy on outsourcing, sales volume, annual budget, number of employees, division structure and types of people it hires, market share, profitability, and location of physical facilities.

- ✔ The section, "Resources for Research: Print Yes, Cyberspace Yes" in this chapter, gives you more information about how to research your next job.

What should you do when a friend wishes to float your resume among clients and colleagues and you don't know where it will land? If you value the friendship and can't persuade your friend that you would appreciate an interview instead, create a general resume reflecting what you most want to do. Complete the worksheets in Part II and then write a resume based on what you'd most like to do, listing the qualifications that support your goal.

When One Resume Will Do — or Has to Do

As I often say, nothing beats a perfect or near-perfect match. Suppose a company sports a job opening requiring A, B, and C experience or education; by designing your resume for the target position, you show that you are well endowed with A, B, and C experience or education — a very close match between their requirements and your qualifications. Welcome to the short list of preferred candidates.

The trouble with creating a custom-tailored resume for every job opening is that many busy and beleaguered people feel as though they can barely manage to get to the dentist for a checkup, buy groceries, pick up the dry cleaning, ship the kids off to school on time, run over to fix Mom's furnace, and generally get through the day — much less write more than one version of an irresistible resume.

It may come down to this: One great resume, or no great resume.

A single version of your resume will usually do when you (a) are a new graduate or (b) have a fairly well defined career path and intend not to color outside the lines of your experience. Even when you allow yourself the luxury of fielding just one resume, you can't put your feet up, watch the sunset, and drink margaritas. With each resume that you distribute, you must attach a personalized cover letter that directly targets the specific job opening. *Cover Letters For Dummies* (from IDG Books Worldwide, Inc., by yours truly) tells you how.

Resources for Research: Print Yes, Cyberspace Yes

A global knowledge revolution, as far-reaching as the Industrial Revolution, is changing business, and business is changing the job market. No one is immune as lifetime jobs become a memory. The good news is that more resources to help us find new work connections have appeared during the past decade than in all of previous history.

By researching the company and industry to customize your resume and determine new job prospects, not only do you gain the firepower to create a KickButt resume, but you also build an arsenal of data points to use later in interviews.

You won't use every scrap of research, of course. Some data will be useful only for impressing your future co-workers at the next office holiday party. The problem is knowing which data will be surplus; glean as much as time and your study habits permit. In general, the higher the level of job you seek, the more research you need to do in order to be seen as the best candidate for the job. Certainly, if you're writing a resume for an above-the-line job that you really want, pull out all the stops.

- ✔ Line up the usual suspects in printed form — directories, newspapers, magazines, trade journals — but go further. Check to see whether your library subscribes to electronic information-retrieval services, such as Nexis, and CD-ROM databases.

- ✔ Travel the Internet, which also may be available at your library, using search engines and indexing services; if this suggestion is beyond your immediate reach, your new best friend should be a geek.

- ✔ If you need a hand with discovering the position's requirements, turn to job descriptions or occupational profiles, which may be available at a large library, on the Internet, or on CD-ROMs designed for home computers. See the "Job descriptions online" sidebar for a list of resources.

The following print references to assist in your job research may be familiar to you. But if you are puzzled by the mentions of World Wide Web sites on the Internet, cyberspace indexing services, search engines, and other online lingo in these listings — and throughout this resume guide — step back and get up to par by reading *Modems For Dummies,* 2nd Edition. *The Internet For Dummies,* 3rd Edition, or *Netscape and the World Wide Web For Dummies,* 2nd Edition, published by IDG Books Worldwide. They cover the essentials of using electronic communications tools.

- Recruitment ads printed in newspapers and trade periodicals not only flag growing companies but identify benchmark industry requirements. Don't overlook local business journals.

- Library business resources are useful and include literally hundreds of directories. Ask a librarian at the nearest large library which of its references are current. Among the best known:

    - *Corporate Jobs Outlook!*

    - *Gale's Job Seeker's Guide to Private and Public Companies*

    - *Hoover's Handbook of American Companies*

    - *The Million Dollar Directory*

    - *Moody's Complete Corporate Index*

    - *Standard & Poor's Registry of Corporations, Directors and Executives*

    - *The Thomas Registers*

    - *Infotrac,* a library computer-based indexing system for locating business articles by company name and subject area

- Company annual reports speak volumes about a publicly traded company, but printed copies are costly. Company investor relations departments are no longer as willing to mail them to job seekers as they once were. If you can't find a collection of annual reports in a library, don't steal a stockbroker's time by pretending that your interest in reports and company research is for investment purposes. That dodge still works, but stockbrokers are rightfully resentful of the practice.

- Use a free cyberspace indexing service, such as Yahoo! (`http://www.yahoo.com`), to find companies hosting Web sites on the Net. In addition to using an indexing service, use a search engine to help you find company information. A clearinghouse for 250 top search engines is the NextBigThing.Search.com. (`http://www.search.com`)

- Edgar (`http://www.sec.gov`) is a free Internet resource to find corporate financial filings to the Securities & Exchange Commission. For any publicly held company, you can uncover such factors as recent financial performance, corporate assets, brands and divisions, and debt structure.

✔ JobWeb (`http://www.jobweb.org`) is a free comprehensive site with lots of company profiles, including everything from management and brand names to future plans. This fabulous site aimed at new college graduates and alumni is lifted into cyberspace by the nonprofit National Association of Colleges and Employers.

✔ AT&T Business Network (for pricing, call 800-660-2299) is a comprehensive resource loaded with information job seekers can use. Access Business Online (`http://www.clickit.com/`) allows you to mouse around company profiles for free; but some links lead to fee-based services.

Entrepreneurs know that some people sell what they can make; others make what they can sell. Behind the simplicity of the statement is a profound concept. After you think about it for a few seconds, you'll realize that there's a corollary in resume writing. Don't be content with merely trying to sell what you can write. Find out what employers want when hiring for your field — find out what sells.

The KickButt resume approach means that you write what you can sell. Research helps you find what you have that sells.

Job descriptions online

Here are some resources for finding out more about a position's requirements:

✔ Try a software store for *Descriptions Now!,* a major but modestly priced CD-ROM database of 2,800 job descriptions that you can buy.

✔ Occupational profiles, although not job descriptions, are free online and can remind you of what functions to mention on your resume; of several sites displaying occupational profiles from the federal Labor Department's *Occupational Outlook Handbook,* America Online's Careers forum is among the easiest to use. A print version of the Handbook is available in most libraries.

✔ Libraries may offer major career guidance databases such as *Gale's Career Guidance System* on CD-ROM, which includes occupational briefs.

Pumping iron research

Here's an unusual exercise to sharpen your resume writing skills. It comes from Nick Corcodilos, author of *The New Interview Instruction Book* and host of America Online's *Ask the Headhunter Forum* (AOL keyword: headhunter):

Practice writing a resume that does not mention your academic credentials or work experience (previous employers or job titles).

This is no joke. If you follow this exercise, all that your resume will include is the needs of the employer. The purpose of the exercise is to encourage you to thoroughly research the company so that you can write your material in terms of the work that the employer needs done and explain to the employer how you will do that work profitably.

(On your real resume, you will, of course, include your past history. This is just an exercise.)

Write Until It's Right

Can you write a decent resume in nanoseconds? Several recent resume books sport titles insisting that you can do just about that. Bogus! A well-developed resume requires adequate curing time to form, mellow, and develop as you recall think, write, think some more, rewrite, proofread, get feedback, and rewrite.

All too many job hunters scatter hundreds of thrown-together resumes. Then they wait. Nothing happens. Why do you think nobody bothers to call with an interview offer? Does thrown-together too often get thrown out?

If you don't want to be left behind because of a thrown together resume, write a KickButt resume. It works. By now, you may be wondering which format to use. The fact is, any format can be molded into a KickButt resume. Chapter 2 displays a selection of resume formats and suggests which ones may hold the most promise for you.

After tailoring your KickButt resume, must you also customize a cover letter? Here's the wrong answer: No, just roll out the old I-saw-your-ad-and-I-am-enclosing-my-resume cliché. Here's the right answer: Yes, a tailored cover letter is the perfect sales tool for a tailored resume.

But that's a topic for another book. (Check out *Cover Letters For Dummies* for everything you need to know about cover letters and more.)

Chapter 2

Finding Your Best Format

. . . .

In This Chapter

▶ Choosing from an extensive format lineup

▶ Using handy templates

▶ Comparing format features

▶ Tips on choosing your best format

. . . .

Resume format refers not to the design or look of your resume but to how you organize and emphasize your information. *Different format styles flatter different histories.* This chapter helps you choose a format that headlines your strengths and hides your shortcomings.

If you've been in the job wars, resume formats focus your hard-news reporting of the forts you've captured, the flags you've flown, and the good conduct medals you're entitled to wear. If you don't have a track record of achievements, accomplishments, and quantifiable results yet — if you just got out of school and haven't been to job boot camp — your resume's format impacts how long you will serve in the unemployed ranks, so pay attention.

An extensive lineup of resume formats follows. A template you can use for developing your own resume illustrates each. Reconnoiter the lot of them before deciding *which best tells your story.*

Resume Formats

The three basic resume styles are

✔ Reverse chronological

✔ Functional

✔ Hybrid (also called *combination*)

These basic styles have spawned a variety of other formats:

- Accomplishment
- Curriculum vitae, academic
- Curriculum vitae, international
- KeyWord
- Linear
- Portfolio
- Professional
- Targeted

Table 2-1 gives you a breakdown of which format to use when.

Table 2-1 Choosing Your Best Resume Format at a Glance

Your Situation	Formats to Try
Perfect career pattern	Reverse chronological, targeted
Rookie or ex-military	Functional, hybrid, accomplishment, targeted, linear
Seasoned ace	Functional, hybrid, accomplishment, KeyWord
Computer friendly	KeyWord
Business	Reverse chronological, accomplishment, targeted
Technical	KeyWord, targeted, accomplishment
Professional	Professional, academic curriculum vitae, portfolio
Government	Reverse chronological, professional
Arts/teaching	Professional, portfolio, academic curriculum vitae
Job history gaps	Functional, hybrid, accomplishment, targeted
Multitrack job history	Functional, hybrid, targeted, KeyWord
Career change	Functional, KeyWord, targeted
International job seeker	International curriculum vitae
Special issues	Functional, hybrid, targeted

Why the reverse chronological format is the heavy favorite

Recruiters and other RezReaders prefer the joy of a chronological job-by-job retelling of your experience because it's a fast read and permits them to spot flaws easily.

Screening *out* all but the very best candidates in a pool is the recruiter's job; screening yourself *into* the candidate pool is your job. When your story cannot best be told in a reverse chronological resume, don't roll over and go chronological just because recruiters favor the style.

You and the recruiter don't have the same goals on this issue. The recruiter wants to screen out quickly. But you want the recruiter to take a second look. Presenting your qualifications in the most flattering format best displays your experience and talents, possibly getting you into that *in* pool that the recruiter would otherwise have taken you out of.

At root, formats come in three[1] family trees: The *reverse chronological* lists all employment and education, beginning with the most recent and working backward. The skills-based *functional* shouts what you can do instead of relaying what you've done and where you did it. The *hybrid* or *combination* is a marriage of both formats. Take a close look at each of these three progenitors before you examine their saplings.

Note: The narrative format is a chronological format starting with the oldest facts and working forward to the newest facts. It's old-fashioned. A pretentious variation of the narrative format uses the third person as though you were writing a biography.

Reverse Chronological Format

The reverse chronological (RC) format is straightforward: It cites your employments from the most recent back, showing dates as well as employers and educational institutions (college, vocational-technical schools, and career-oriented programs and courses). You accent a steady work history with a clear pattern of upward or lateral mobility.

---

[1] Some famous, wise, and savvy resume gurus say reverse chronological and functional are the only two resume styles. They don't count hybrid styles. But what do they know?

Strengths:

- This format is by far the most popular with employers and recruiters because it seems so, well, up-front.

- RC links employment dates, underscoring continuity. The weight of your experience confirms that you are a "social service," "technical," or other career specialist.

- RC positions you for the next upward career step.

- As the most traditional of formats, RC fits traditional industries (like banking, education, accounting).

Weaknesses:

- When previous job titles are at variance with the target position, this format does not support the objective. Without careful management, it reveals everything, including inconsequential jobs and negative factors.

- RC can spotlight periods of unemployment or brief job tenure.

- Without careful management, RC reveals your age.

- Without careful management, RC may suggest that you were plateaued in a job too long.

Who should use this format and who should think twice

Use the RC if you fall into any of these categories:

- You have a steady school and work record reflecting constant growth or lateral movement.

- Your most recent employer is a respected name in the industry, and the name may ease your entry into a new position.

- Your most recent job titles are impressive stepping-stones.

- You're a KickButt-savvy writer who knows how to manage potential negative factors, such as inconsequential jobs, too few jobs, too many temporary jobs, too many years at the same job, or too many years of age.

Reverse chronological format

YOUR NAME
Home Address
City, State, Zip Code
(###) ###-#### (Telephone)   (###) ###-#### (Fax)
###@###.# (E-mail)

Objective:
A position that uses your skills.

SUMMARY
- Number of years of work experience, paid and unpaid, relevant to target position
- Achievement that proves you can handle the target
- Another achievement that proves you can handle the target
- Skills, traits, characteristics -- facts that further your ability to handle the target
- Education and training relating to the target (if unrelated, bury in resume body)

PROFESSIONAL EXPERIENCE AND ACCOMPLISHMENTS

19## - Present   Job Title   Employer, Employer's Location
A brief synopsis of your purpose in the company, detailing essential functions, products and customer base you managed.
- An achievement in this position relevant to objective (do not repeat summary)
- A second achievement in this position relevant to current objective
- More accomplishments, i.c., awards, recognition, promotion, raise, praise, training

19## - 19##   Job Title   Employer, Employer's Location
Detailed as above.

19## - 19##   Job Title   Employer, Employer's Location
A briefer synopsis of your purpose in the company, overviewing functions, products, customer base.
- An achievement made during this position relevant to current objective
- More accomplishments, i.e. awards, recognition, promotion, raise, praise, training

19## - 19##   Job Title   Employer, Employer's Location
An even briefer synopsis of your purpose in the company, overviewing functions, products, customer base.
- An achievement made during this position that's relevant to current objective

EDUCATION AND PROFESSIONAL TRAINING

Degree(s), classes, seminars, educational awards and honors
Credentials, clearances, licenses

Here's who should think twice:

✔ Young people with anorexic employment histories may not do fabulously with this format. Listing a stray student job or two is not persuasive even when you open with superb educational credentials that are even better with internships and co-op experiences. Rookies, with careful attention, you can do a credible job on an RC by extracting from your extracurricular activities every shred of skills, which you present as abilities to do work with extraordinary commitment and a head for quick learning.

✔ People with work history problems — gaps, demotions, stagnation in a single position, job hopping through four jobs in three years, reentering the work force after a break to raise a family — must exercise very careful management to truthfully modify stark realities. Other formats may serve you better.

✔ This is not the format of choice for career changers or people who have significant work history problems — ex-inmates and people who have experienced mental disabilities, for example.

Who says a reverse chronological resume can't be sexy?

Three tiny color logos seeded in an otherwise plain reverse chronological resume for a former-Marine-turned-new-college-graduate appealed mightily to a food-processing plant in Evansville, Indiana. The dime-sized logos were those of the Marine Corps, the University of Southern Indiana, and St. Mary's Medical Center, where the graduate worked while in school.

I usually discourage resume logos because the ones I've seen are about as tasteful as bumper stickers and, technologically speaking, accident prone (meltdown occurs when job computers meet resume graphics).

This logo-laden reverse chronological resume must have had star power, however, which proves that exceptions exist for every opinion. USI Career Services and Placement Assistant Director Tracy Powers says that not only was the new graduate tapped from an applicant pool of 2,000, but he was wooed with a top-dollar offer. "When the new graduate was offered a $25,000 management position, he said thanks but his current salary was $28K. They came back with a $38K offer and hired him."

Instructions

The KickButt way to create an RC is as follows:

✔ Focus on areas of specific relevance to your target position or career field.

✔ List all pertinent places worked, including for each the name of the employer and the city in which you worked, the years you were there, your title, your responsibilities, and your measurable achievements.

✔ The RC template included in this chapter is generic and does not show how to handle problems. You can group problems in a second work history section under a heading of *Other Experience* or *Previous Experience,* or *Related Experience.*

Functional Format

The functional format is a resume of ability-focused topics — portable skills or functional areas. It ignores chronological order. In its purest form, the functional style omits dates, employers, and job titles. Employers do not like absence of particulars, which is why contemporary functional resumes list employers, job titles, and sometimes dates — but still downplay this information by briefly listing it at the bottom of the resume. The functional format is oriented toward what the job seeker can do for the employer instead of narrating history.

Strengths:

✔ A functional resume directs a RezReader's eyes to what you want noticed. It helps a reader visualize what you can do instead of locking into a rigid perspective of when and where you learned to do it. Functional resumes salute the future rather than embalm the past.

✔ The functional format — written after researching the target company — serves up the precise functions or skills that the employer wants. It's like saying, "You want budget control and turn-around skills — I have budget control and turn-around skills." The skills sell is a magnet to RezReader eyes!

✔ It uses unpaid and nonwork experience to your best advantage.

✔ It allows you to eliminate or subordinate work history that does not support your current objective.

Weaknesses:

- Because recruiters and employers are more accustomed to RC formats, departing from the norm may raise suspicion that you're not the cream of the crop of applicants. They may assume that you're trying to hide inadequate experience, educational deficits, or who knows what.

- Functional styles may leave unclear which skills grew from which jobs or experiences.

- A clear career path is not obvious.

- This format does not maximize recent coups in the job market.

Who should use this format and who should think twice

This resume is heaven-sent for career changers, new graduates, ex-military personnel, seasoned aces, and individuals with multitrack job histories, work history gaps, or special-issue problems.

Job seekers with blue-ribbon backgrounds and managers and professionals who are often tapped by executive recruiters should avoid this format.

Instructions

Choose areas of expertise that you have acquired during the course of your career, including education and unpaid activities. These areas become skill and functional headings, which vary by the target position or career field. Achievements are noted below each heading. A few examples of headings follow: *Management, Sales, Budget Control, Cost Cutting, Project Implementation, Turn-Around Successes.*

List the headings in the order of importance. Use a series of short statements when grouping your skills. Turn your statements into power hitters with measurable achievements.

Functional format

YOUR NAME
Address, City, State, Zip Code
(###) ###-#### (Telephone), (###) ###-#### (Fax)
###@###.## (E-mail)

Job Title You Desire

More than (# years paid and unpaid) work experience, in target area, contributing to an (achievement/result/high ranking in industry/top 5% of performance reviews). Add accomplishments, strengths, proficiencies, characteristics, education, brief testimonial -- anything that supports your target job title.

PROFESSIONAL EXPERIENCE AND ACCOMPLISHMENTS

A TOP SKILL (Pertinent to objective)
- An achievement illustrating this skill, and the location/employer of this skill *
- A second achievement illustrating this skill, and the location/employer of this skill *

A SECOND TOP SKILL (Pertinent to objective)
- An achievement illustrating this skill, and the location/employer of this skill *
- A second achievement illustrating this skill, and the location/employer of this skill *

A THIRD TOP SKILL (Pertinent to objective)
- An achievement illustrating this skill, and the location/employer of this skill *
- An achievement illustrating this skill, and the location/employer of this skill *

A FOURTH SKILL (Optional -- must relate to objective)
- Detailed as above

A UNIQUE AREA OF PROFICIENCY (Pertinent to objective)
- An achievement testifying to this proficiency, including the location/employer *
- A list of equipment, processes, software, or terms you know that reflect your familiarity with this area of proficiency
- A list of training experiences that document your proficiency

EMPLOYMENT HISTORY

19## - Present	**Job Title**	Employer, Location
19## - 19##	**Job Title**	Employer, Location
19## - 19##	**Job Title**	Employer, Location
19## - 19##	**Job Title**	Employer, Location

PROFESSIONAL TRAINING AND EDUCATION
Degrees, Credentials, Clearances, Licenses, Classes, Seminars, Training

* Omit locations/employers if your work history is obviously lacking in lockstep upward mobility

Templates: pro and con

Some resume advisers argue that people who use a model template reflect no ingenuity and independence, somehow forecasting future robotic behavior on the job. Lumping qualifications into a mold not parallel to the individual's background proves that the applicant is lazy, template critics say.

Other resume advisers diagnose the anti-template crowd as being out of their cotton-pickin' minds. Template advocates applaud predesigned formats. They appreciate applicants' abilities to use expert advice; these applicants show that they can follow by example but know how to channel their selling points. As one adviser says, "Everyone tweaks templates a bit. Why reinvent the wheel?"

Templates are guides, not handcuffs — you're not locked into anything.

Hybrid Format

The hybrid, a combination of reverse chronological and functional formats, satisfies demands for timelines as well as showcases your marketable skills and impressive accomplishments. Many people find the hybrid — or one of its offspring — the most attractive of all formats.

Essentially, in a hybrid, a functional summary tops a reverse chronological presentation of dates, employers, and capsules of each position's duties.

The hybrid style is similar to the contemporary functional format — so much so that making a case for distinction is sometimes difficult.

Strength: A hybrid format combines the strengths of both the reverse chronological and functional formats.

Weakness: A hybrid style contains more "frills" than a very conservative RezReader may prefer.

Who should use this format and who should think twice

The hybrid is a wise choice for rookies, ex-military personnel, seasoned aces, those with job history gaps or a multitrack job history, and individuals with special-issue problems.

Hybrid format

YOUR NAME
Address, City, State, Zip Code
(###) ###-#### (Telephone)   (###) ###-#### (Fax)
###@###.## (E-mail)

Objective: Position as_____using your___ (#) years of experience in skills key to target.

SUMMARY OF QUALIFICATIONS
Number of years in area of target position
Related education, training and accreditation
An achievement pertinent to objective
Traits that reinforce your candidacy for this position
Other accomplishments, characteristics, proficiencies

SUMMARY OF SKILLS
• Technical skills   • Processes   • Computer software

ACCOMPLISHMENTS AND EXPERIENCE

Job Title, Top Proficiencies Used   Employer, Location

A Top Skill (Pertinent to objective)
• Accomplishments made while in this position
• Several apt achievements from position, pertinent to this skill and the objective
Another Skill (Pertinent to objective)
• Several achievements pertinent to this skill and the objective

19## - Present

Job Title, Top Proficiencies Used   Employer, Location

A Top Skill (Pertinent to objective)
• Accomplishments made while in this position, even more detailed
• Several apt achievements from this position, similar to above
Another Skill (Pertinent to objective)
• Several apt achievements from position, pertinent to this skill and the objective
19## - 19##

Job Title, Top Proficiencies Used   Employer, Location

A Top Skill (Pertinent to objective)
• Accomplishments made while in this position
• Several apt achievements from position, pertinent to this skill and the objective
Another Skill (Pertinent to objective)
• Several achievements pertinent to this skill and the objective
19## - 19##

PROFESSIONAL TRAINING AND EDUCATION
Degrees, accreditations, licenses, clearances, courses

Career changers or job seekers needing more appropriate formats, such as functional or portfolio, should skip the hybrid.

Instructions

Build a functional format of ability-focused topics and add employment documentation — employers, locations, dates, and duties.

Accomplishment Format

Definitely not a boring read, an accomplishment format immediately moves your strongest marketing points to center stage, grabs the reader's interest, and doesn't let go. As a rapper might intone: Use flash and dash to go for cash.

A sapling to the hybrid resume, the accomplishment format banners both qualifications *and* accomplishments. This is the format of choice for many executives, particularly in traditionally mobile industries, such as advertising, communications, and publishing.

Strength: This format offers benefits similar to those of functional and hybrid styles noted earlier.

Weakness: Readers who prefer a reverse chronological style may view the accomplishment format as too jazzed up.

Who should use this format and who should think twice

Here's when to use the accomplishment format:

- ✔ The same people who consider functional and hybrid styles should look at this one: career changers, new graduates, ex-military personnel, seasoned aces, and individuals with multitrack job histories, work history gaps, or special-issue problems. The accomplishment presentation is especially effective for individuals whose work history may not have been smooth but was, at times, bright with great successes.
- ✔ Individuals returning to payroll status after a period of self-employment find this format effective.

People who have climbed career steps without a stumble should use a reverse chronological instead of the accomplishment.

Accomplishment format

YOUR NAME

Address   Telephone Number: (###) ###-####
City, State, Zip Code   E-Mail: #####@##.##
                                 Message and/or Fax Number(s): (###) ###-####

OBJECTIVE
Position as___using skills and experience accumulated over __(#) years.

QUALIFICATIONS
- Number of years of experience that is pertinent to objective
- Your record of improvement or reputation in the industry
- Specific skills and training apt to objective
- Areas of specialized proficiency
- Work ethic traits demonstrating candidacy and constructiveness

SKILLS
- Equipment familiarities
- Procedural familiarities
- Terminology familiarities
- Technological familiarities

ACCOMPLISHMENTS
In any order, list accomplishments (quantifying with numbers and percentages when appropriate) that elaborate such achievements as

- competitive skills, technological proficiency, professional aptness
- improvements, innovations
- revenue-saving strategies
- promotions, raises
- increasing responsibilities, management and troubleshooting functions
- praise from employers and/or coworkers
- training rendered, training received

PROFESSIONAL EXPERIENCE
• Job Title	Employer, Location	19## - 19##
• Job Title	Employer, Location	19## - 19##
• Job Title	Employer, Location	19## - 19##
• Job Title	Employer, Location	19## - 19##

EDUCATION
Academic and professional accreditation(s), major(s), minor(s), emphasis
Universities, schools, and courses attended or in progress

Formats to use when the executive recruiter calls

Executive recruiting is usually a response to an employer's known problem in a given business area. Accomplishment formats, along with reverse chronological and targeted styles, are well equipped to tell employers how you can solve their problems.

When an executive recruiter calls, ask for enough details about the position's problem areas to give you ammunition for whipping out a made-to-order resume. If you're a candidate, the recruiter may be happy to have as many as four *readable* pages about your background, as long as you grab attention on the first page. Remember that most executive decision makers favor reverse-chronological presentations, so use conservative language in drawing attention to your accomplishments on this format. See Chapter 4 for more information about the language of resumes.

Instructions

List accomplishments in order of importance, making chronology a secondary factor. Close with a summarized reverse chronological work history.

Targeted Format

A targeted format, tailored to a given job, is VIP (very important person) treatment. Targeting is persuasive because everyone likes to be given the VIP treatment.

The targeted style is written to match point-for-point a specific job that is offered by a specific employer.

The template in this chapter is but one way to build a targeted resume. You can equally benefit with other format options springing from the functional or hybrid branches of the resume family. You choose.

Strength: The targeted format shows the employer that you're a good match for the position.

Weakness: You may not be readily considered for other jobs.

Targeted format

YOUR NAME
Address, City, State, Zip Code
Telephone (###) ###-####, Fax (###) ###-####
E-Mail ###@###.####

Objective: Position as_____(title of job employer offers) using your___ (#) years
of experience in skills essential and specialized to the position.

SUMMARY OF QUALIFICATIONS

- Number of years in area of target, explaining similarities to objective position/duties
- Related education, training, accreditation -- specifically those employer will appreciate
- An achievement directly related to target
- Traits reinforcing your candidacy for this position, specifically those employer requires
- Other accomplishments, characteristics, knowledge either rare or prized in the field

SUMMARY OF SKILLS

•Technical Skills Employer Wants
•Processes Employer Uses
•Computer and Software Skills Employer Needs

ACCOMPLISHMENTS AND EXPERIENCE

Job Title   Employer, Location   19## - Present

   A Top Skill (Pertinent to objective)

- Accomplishments made in this position targeting the employer's priorities or customer base

- Several other apt achievements from position, pertinent to skill and objective

   Another Top Skill (Pertinent to objective)

- Several apt achievements pertinent to this skill and the objective

Job Title   Employer, Location   19## - 19##
Details as above

Job Title   Employer, Location   19## - 19##
Details as above

PROFESSIONAL TRAINING AND EDUCATION
Degrees, accreditations, licenses, clearances, courses

When resumes and research are beyond reach

You say you're not sure you want to do enough research on a position to write a targeted resume? Definitely not a KickButt mind-set, but you're still ahead of an applicant who wrote the following query to the human resources department of a big company (I did not make this up):

Dear Sirs, I would very much like to send a resume to you, but I haven't the slightest idea how to fill out a resume, and I can't remember the dates or addresses for any of it anyway. So if that is going to keep me from being employed by your company, then to h—with it! Otherwise, call me in for an interview and a job.

Who should use this format and who should think twice

Pretty much everyone kicks butt with a targeted resume. Ex-military personnel can translate militaryspeak to civilianese, rookies can equate their nonpaid experience to employer requirements, and seasoned aces can reach deep into their backgrounds to show, item for item, how they qualify. This format is a reasoned choice for people with strong work histories but a few zits here and there.

The targeted format is not a great idea for anyone who is lazy about doing research — the success of the targeted resume depends on your lining up data ducks in advance.

Instructions

Find out what the position demands and — fact for fact — write how you offer exactly those goods. If you can meet better than 80 percent of the position's requirements, you've got a shot at an interview; if less than 80 percent, don't give up breathing while you wait for your telephone to ring.

Linear Format

A linear format (line by line — hence, *linear*) tells your story in the short spurts of benefits (achievements, winning moves) that you offer. An offspring of the reverse chronological format, the linear doesn't get into great detail; it sparks curiosity to meet you and find out more.

Linear format

YOUR NAME
Address, City, State, Zip Code
(###) ###-#### (Telephone), (###) ###-#### (Fax)
###@###.### (E-mail)

QUALIFICATIONS SUMMARY

- Number of years of work experience, paid and unpaid, pertinent to objective position
- Accomplishment(s) that prove your unique candidacy for this position
- Skills geared for the objective position or company
- Other things the employer will like to know -- proficiencies, characteristics, achievements, training, credentials and education

PROFESSIONAL EXPERIENCE AND ACCOMPLISHMENTS

19## - Present   Job Title   Employer, Employer's Location

- An achievement made during this position that is pertinent to current objective, detailing job skills and responsibilities

- A second achievement made during this position also pertinent to current objective

- More accomplishments -- that is, awards, recognition, promotion, raise, praise, training

* Divide description according to titles held with employer, listing titles as subheadings.

19## - 19##   Job Title   Employer, Employer's Location

Same details as above.

* Divide description according to titles held with employer, listing titles as subheadings.

19## - 19##   Job Title   Employer, Employer's Location

Same details as above.

* Divide description according to titles held with employer, listing titles as subheadings.

EDUCATION AND PROFESSIONAL TRAINING

Degree(s), university, year
Major
Top achievement

* Include other seminars, awards, honors, credentials, clearances, licenses.

COMMUNITY LEADERSHIP

Memberships and other offices in community organizations

This spaced-out variation of the reverse chronological format lacks a job objective section and opens with a skills summary instead. Plenty of white space is the hallmark of this achievement-highlighted document.

Career advisers pin a blue ribbon on this format.

Strengths:

✔ Linears are very easy to read quickly, particularly in a stack of resumes a foot high. Instant readability is increasingly important as harried RezReaders struggle with the clock and baby boomers become middle-aged RezReaders whose eyes do not enjoy poring over pages sagging with text.

✔ Because the format presents your starring events in a line-by-line visual presentation, your achievements are not likely to be overlooked as they would if buried deep in a text paragraph.

Weakness: You can't pack as much information into a linear (remember the white space), but you can pack plenty of sell.

Who should use this format and who should think twice

This format works to showcase career progression — steady as you go. If that's you, use the linear.

Job seekers with gaps in employment, too many jobs, few advancements, or scant experience and those who have seen enough sunrises to be on the shady side of 50 should avoid the linear.

Instructions

Write down your achievements and other necessary data, look at the big lumps of text, and then divide and conquer. Think white space.

Professional Format

A professional format, also called a professional vitae, is slightly long-winded (say, 3 to 5 pages) but factual. It emphasizes professional qualifications and activities. This format is essentially a shortened academic curriculum vitae.

Professional format

YOUR NAME
Address, City, State, Zip Code
(###) ###-#### (Telephone), (###) ###-#### (Fax)
###@###.### (E-mail)

EDUCATION AND PROFESSIONAL TRAINING

Degrees, credentials, awards, achievements, honors, seminars, clearances, licenses.

OBJECTIVE: A position that uses your talents, with an emphasis on your special skills.

SUMMARY

• Number of years of work experience, paid and unpaid, relevant to target

• Accomplishment(s) that prove your unique candidacy for this position

• Strengths geared for the objective position or company

• Other things the employer will like to know -- proficiencies, characteristics, achievements, training, credentials and education

PROFESSIONAL EXPERIENCE AND ACCOMPLISHMENTS

19## - Present   Job Title   Employer, Employer's Location

A brief synopsis of your purpose in the company, detailing essential functions and products you managed, and your customer base.

- An achievement made during position pertinent to target

- A second achievement made during position also pertinent to target

- More achievements -- awards, recognition, promotion, raise, praise, training

19## - 19##   Job Title   Employer, Employer's Location

An even briefer synopsis of your purpose in the company, overviewing functions, products, customer base.

- An achievement made during this position that is applicable to target

- More achievements -- awards, recognition, promotion, raise, praise, training

* *List three previous jobs with the same detail as above; divide jobs according to job title, not employer.*

Strength: The professional resume is mandatory for certain kinds of positions; your choice is whether to send this type or go all the way and send an academic curriculum vitae.

Weakness: Professional resumes are reviewed under a microscope; every deficiency stands out. Adding a portfolio that shows your experience-based work skills may compensate for missing chunks of formal requirements. Just be sure that any unsolicited samples you send are KickButt quality and need no explanation.

Who should use this format and who should think twice

Professionals in medicine, science, and law should use this format. Also use it when common sense or convention makes it the logical choice.

For most nonprofessionals, especially managers, the professional format is tedious.

Should you send two resumes at one time?

Now that job computers sit up late at night reading resumes, people ask whether they should send two copies — a computer-friendly, no-graphics style (described in Chapter 1 and later in this chapter in the KeyWord format discussion) and a paper resume with fancier fonts and decorative designs that are attractive to human eyes but turn computers green.

Although the idea of getting your money's worth out of a stamp by sending both types is tempting, a minisurvey of human resources managers suggests that you send only one resume per company. Their argument is that two resumes create too much work for the human resources department.

So which type of resume do you send? Call ahead to see whether the company scans resumes. If it does, or if you can't find out, send only the computer-friendly resume. If you know that scanning isn't used at a particular company, send the paper resume that will appeal to human eyes. A linear resume is an agreeable choice for both paper and computers. Also look at the KeyWord format.

Instructions

Begin with education, professional training, and an objective. Follow with a summary of main points that you want the reader to absorb. Follow with details of your professional experience and accomplishments.

Follow the template in this chapter, paying attention to accomplishments. Just because you present yourself in a low-key, authoritative manner does not mean that you can forget to say how good you are.

KeyWord Format

Any resume can be a KeyWord resume. It becomes a KeyWord resume when you add a *profile of KeyWords* (nouns identifying your qualifications — see Chapter 4) anywhere on any type of format. I like front-loading a KeyWord preface at the top of the resume.

The template shown in this chapter is a format that works well for computer scanning. Support your KeyWords with facts but do not repeat the exact phrasing in a KeyWord profile and in other parts of your resume — vary your language. Repetition must be handled with thought.

Strength: Virtually everyone benefits from using a KeyWord profile — it functions like a skills summary. Job seekers sending resumes by e-mail or postings on the Internet should always include KeyWords.

Weakness: A minority of recruiters dislike a KeyWord preface. Their objection: "It appears to be a check-box–oriented approach to doing a resume." It's not a weakness that's likely to get you rejected out-of-hand, however. If the body of the resume supports your KeyWords (which it should if it's KickButt quality), and you can do only one resume, it's worth the risk.

Who should use this format and and who should think twice

Most job seekers should consider the KeyWord option. Resumes of technical people can't leave home without it.

However, top management executives (the $500,000-a-year-and-up kind) are unlikely to be recruited from resume databases. Executive recruiters do, however, construct their own in-house databases. In building these in-house databases, they may import from public-domain databases that input information from traditional resumes and other sources.

KeyWord format

YOUR NAME, Address, City, State, Zip Code
(###) ###-#### (Telephone), (###) ###-#### (Fax),
###@###.### (E-mail)

KeyWords: General nouns, phrases, and terminology known to be valued in the position and industry; specific KeyWords descriptive of duties and proficiencies necessary to position; specific terms known to be priority to employer/company you're applying to, including credentials, years of experience, areas of familiarity, and equipment involved

Objective: Title of opening, using the following highlights of your background:
• Number of years of work experience, paid and unpaid, relevant to target
• Accomplishment(s) that prove your unique candidacy for this position
• Strengths geared for the objective position or company, education, credentials and training

PROFESSIONAL EXPERIENCE AND ACCOMPLISHMENTS

19## - Present	**Employer, Employer's Location**

Present Job Title
A brief synopsis of your purpose in the company, detailing essential functions and products you rendered, and customer base.
• An achievement made during position appropriate to current objective
• A second achievement made during position also apt to objective
• More achievements, awards, recognition, promotion, raise, praise
• Equipment used, processes, procedures, in noun form

19## - 19##	**Employer, Employer's Location**

Job Title
* Same details as above.

19## - 19##	**Employer, Employer's Location**

Job Title
A briefer synopsis of your purpose, similar to previous job.
• An achievement made during position pertinent to current objective
• A second achievement made during position that's a priority in current objective
• Equipment used, processes, procedures, in noun form

19## - 19##	**Employer, Employer's Location**

Job Title
An even briefer synopsis of position, overviewing functions, products, customer base.
• An achievement made during position pertinent to current objective
• Equipment used, processes, procedures, in noun form

EDUCATION AND PROFESSIONAL TRAINING
Degrees, classes, seminars, awards, achievements, honors, credentials, clearances, licenses

---

Tips for resumes likely to be electronically scanned

- ✔ Put your name and contact information at the top of your resume.

- ✔ Use white or light-colored paper printed on one side.

- ✔ Provide a laser-printed original if possible.

- ✔ Do not fold or staple.

- ✔ Use standard typefaces like Helvetica and Times Roman.

- ✔ Do not use a two-column format.

- ✔ Avoid graphics and boxes.

- ✔ Avoid underlining and shadows.

- ✔ Put parentheses around telephone area codes.

- ✔ Put e-mail addresses on a separate line, or leave plenty of white space in front. A numeric e-mail address should be on a separate line to avoid confusion with the street address.

- ✔ List employers before achievements.

- ✔ Connect dates horizontally (19XX-19XX), not vertically.

- ✔ Spell out words such as *temporary* (not *temp*).

Instructions

As the KeyWord template shows, you begin with your contact information, followed by a KeyWord profile, followed by an objective, several strengths, and reverse chronological employment history.

You may choose not to use a front-loaded KeyWord profile but to use instead a one-paragraph qualifications summary or a skills section composed of brief (one- or two-line) statements. The more KeyWords (or skills) in your resume, the better your chances of being summoned for an interview.

Academic Curriculum Vitae (CV)

The academic CV is a comprehensive biographical statement, typically three to ten pages, emphasizing professional qualifications and activities. A CV of six to eight pages, ten at the most, is recommended for a veteran professional; two to four pages is appropriate for a young professional just starting out (see the professional format).

If your CV is more than four pages long, show mercy and save eyesight by attaching an *executive summary* page to the top. An executive summary gives a brief overview of your qualifications and experience.

Among various possible organizations, the academic CV template (a sapling of the hybrid format but with exhaustive coverage) illustrates a lineup of your contact information, objective, qualifications summary, skills summary, and professional background.

Academic Curriculum Vitae format

YOUR NAME
Curriculum Vitae
Address, City, State, Zip Code
(###) ###-#### (Telephone), (###) ###-#### (Fax)
###@###.### (E-mail address)

Objective (optional): Position as_____(title of position employer offers) using ___ (#) years of experience in _____ (skills essential and specialized to the position).

SUMMARY OF QUALIFICATIONS

- A summary of your education, proficiencies, and career pertinent to target
- Number of years in objective area, explaining similarities to job and its responsibilities
- Related education, training, and accreditation, reflecting employer's goals/ priorities
- An achievement directly related to target
- Traits reinforcing your candidacy for this position, specifically those asked for by the employer and those generally in demand in the field
- Other accomplishments, characteristics, knowledge either rare or prized in the field

SUMMARY OF SKILLS

•Topics of Specialty or Innovation within Field •Areas of Particular Familiarity
•Software Equipment •Processes •Terminology Relevant to Target •Languages

PROFESSIONAL BACKGROUND
EDUCATION
Degrees:
    Ph.D., institution, date of degree (or anticipated date), specialization
    M.A./M.S., institution, date of degree, major, minor, emphasis, concentration
    B.A./B.S., institution, date of degree, major, minor
Courses: Those taken, honors, seminars, number of units, G.P.A. (if a recent graduate)
Other Accreditations: Licenses, clearances
Academic Achievements: Appointments, nominations, leaderships, scholarships, grants, awards, praise, scores, recognitions, accomplishments
Affiliations: Societies, associations, clubs, fraternities, sororities, leagues, memberships

PH.D. DISSERTATION
    Title, advisor, director
    Abstract summary (4-5 sentences) discussing content and methodology

HONORS, AWARDS, AND ACHIEVEMENTS
Appointments, nominations, leaderships, awards, praise, scores, recognitions, accomplishments, high scores, grades, G.P.A.s, fellowships, scholarships, grants, (including B.A./B.S.)

TEACHING EXPERIENCE

Job Title, Top Proficiencies Used   Employer, Location   **19## - Present**

A Top Responsibility (Relevant to objective)
• Accomplishments made in this position targeting the employer's priorities/mission
• Several other achievements from this position, pertinent to objective
Another Skill (Appropriate to objective)
• Several achievements from this position, pertinent to objective

* *Repeat above pattern for each position.*

RESEARCH EXPERIENCE
Positions, locations, dates, descriptions of research in pertinence to target position

TEACHING INTERESTS
Discipline, certification

RESEARCH INTERESTS
Areas of inquiry

PUBLICATIONS
* List all those you are willing to show the search committee
* Include work in progress or pending
* Cite works as follows:

•**"Title of work,"** Name of publication/publisher (*Newsletter, Newspaper, Magazine, Journal, Book*), location of publisher (state & city or major city), date of publication, volume number (v.##), issue number (#.#), series number (#.#.#), page numbers (# - #) (type quotes around the title of your article).

PRESENTATIONS AND PUBLIC APPEARANCES
* Include conference papers and research reports
* List as follows:

•**"Title of presentation,"** location of presentation (City, State), Date (19## - 19##); optional synopsis of content and/or purpose of presentation, audience, results, etc.

PROFESSIONAL AFFILIATIONS
A society, association, league, or club with which you associate, position held, 19## - 19##
A society, association, league, or club with which you associate, position held, 19## - 19##
A society, association, league, or club with which you associate, position held, 19## - 19##

RECOMMENDATIONS
Names and contact information of 3-4 references willing to write recommendation letters

CREDENTIALS
Address where the recipient can access your career/placement file

Strength: A CV presents all the best of you.

Weakness: For people with aging eyes, a CV is reading-intensive. More importantly, weaknesses in any area of your professional credentials are relatively easy to spot.

Who should use this format and who should think twice

Anyone working in a Ph.D.-driven environment, such as higher education, think tanks, science, and elite research and development groups, needs to use this format.

Anyone who can avoid using it should do so.

Instructions

Create a comprehensive summary of your professional employment and accomplishments: education, positions, affiliations, honors, memberships, credentials, dissertation title, fields in which comprehensive examinations were passed, full citations of publications and presentations, awards, discoveries, inventions, patents, seminar leadership, foreign languages, courses taught — whatever is valued in your field.

KickButters, I recommend that you read a book or two on writing CVs because even these stereotypically somber documents can be brightened. I like the *Academic Job Search Handbook* by Mary Morris Heiberger (University of Pennsylvania Press, Philadelphia; telephone 800-445-9880) and *The Curriculum Vitae Handbook* by Rebecca Anthony and Gerald Roe (Rudi Publishing, Iowa City; telephone 319-337-5057).

International Curriculum Vitae Format

The international CV is not the same document as an academic CV. Think of an international CV as an excruciatingly detailed resume of between six and eight pages. Although it solicits private information such as your health status that is outlawed in the U.S., the international CV is favored in some nations as a kind of global ticket to employment.

International Curriculum Vitae format

YOUR NAME
Curriculum Vitae
Home Address, City, State, Country, Province, Zip Code
Include international codes:
(###) ###-#### (Telephone) (###) ###-#### (Fax)
###@###.## (E-mail address)

Objective (optional): Position as_____(title of position employer offers) using your___
(#) years of experience in _____ (skills essential and specialized to the position).

SUMMARY OF QUALIFICATIONS

- A summary of your education, proficiencies, and career pertinent to target
- Number of years in area of objective, explaining similarities to it/its responsibilities
- Related education, training, and accreditation, reflecting employer's goals/priorities
- An achievement directly related to target, that the employer needs
- Traits reinforcing your candidacy for this position, specifically those asked for by the employer and those generally in demand in the field
- Other accomplishments, characteristics, knowledge either rare or prized in the field
- Traveling in field, countries visited, improvements made, distinctions, and so forth

SUMMARY OF SKILLS

- Topics of specialty or innovation within field   • Areas of particular familiarity
- Software Equipment   • Processes   • Terminology Relevant to Target   • Languages

PROFESSIONAL BACKGROUND

EMPLOYMENT

Job Title   Employer, Location   **19## - Present**
A Top Responsibility (Relevant to objective)
- Accomplishments made in this position targeting the employer's priorities/mission
- Several other achievements from this position, pertinent to objective

Another Skill (Appropriate to objective)
- Several achievements from this position, pertinent to objective

  * Repeat above pattern for all jobs.

PROFESSIONAL HONORS
All honorary positions, awards, recognitions, or titles, with locations, 19## - 19##

PUBLICATIONS
- **"Title of work,"** Name of publication/publisher (*Newsletter, Newspaper, Magazine, Journal*), location of publisher (country, languages, state & city or major city), date of publication, volume number (v.##), issue number (#.#), series number (#.#.#), page numbers (# - #)

  * Repeat above citation for all publications.

PRESENTATIONS AND PUBLIC APPEARANCES

•**"Title of presentation,"** location of presentation (Country, City, State, Province, Language), Date (19## - 19##); optional synopsis of content and/or purpose of presentation, audience, results, etc.

> * *Repeat above citation for all presentations.*

PROFESSIONAL AFFILIATIONS

All societies, associations, leagues, or clubs, positions held, locations, 19## - 19##

EDUCATION

Degrees: Ph.D., institution, date of degree (or anticipated date), specialization
M.A./M.S., institution, date of degree, major, minor, concentration
B.A./B.S., institution, date of degree, major, minor
* Give equivalents of these degrees in other countries

Courses: Those taken, honors, seminars, number of units, G.P.A. (if a recent graduate)

Other Accreditations: Licenses, clearances

Academic Achievements: Appointments, nominations, leaderships, scholarships, grants, awards, praise, scores, recognitions, accomplishments

Affiliations: Societies, associations, clubs, fraternities, sororities, leagues, memberships

DOCTORAL DISSERTATION

Title, advisor, director
Abstract summary (4-5 sentences) discussing content and methodology

HONORS, AWARDS AND ACHIEVEMENTS

Appointments, nominations, leaderships, awards, praise, scores, recognitions, accomplishments, high scores, grades, G.P.A.s, fellowships, scholarships, grants, (including B.A./B.S/equivalents)

PERSONAL INFORMATION

• A sentence or so that describes personal attributes pertinent to employer's interests. Think positively, omit negatives, and highlight goal-oriented, functional characteristics that promise of a good worker-employer relationship and reliably good work product. Present specific work-related examples of these personality highlights and explain how they are significant to the employer. Without exaggerating, accentuate the positive, and include all favorable quotes from employers and coworkers, members of the clergy, and public service, volunteer organization, nonprofit organization and political officials
• Age, Marital Status (Single, Engaged, Married)
• Hobbies and leisure activities (travel, clubs, sports, athletics, collections, subscriptions)
• Volunteer service, public service

The international CV is usually a reverse chronological format that includes your contact information, qualifications summary, professional background, education, and personal information. Some European countries prefer the chronological format, which lists education and work experience from the furthest back to the present.

Americans should remember that when working overseas for a native employer, they are not protected by Equal Employment Opportunity laws.

Strength: International employment experts say that if you don't use this format, foreign recruiters may think you're hiding something.

Weakness: The international CV format intrudes into private areas of your life.

Who should use this format and who should think twice

Use this format if you're seeking an overseas job and do not object to revealing information that may subject you to discriminatory hiring practices.

Individuals who feel strongly about invasions of privacy or who are not willing to be rejected out of hand because of gender, religion, race, age, or marital status should avoid this format.

Of course, if you want an overseas job and you don't use this format, you may be out of luck unless you're working through an American recruiter. The recruiter can interpret your concerns and negotiate for a bare minimum of personal information. Nationals of countries other than the U.S. can also use this technique.

Instructions

Formality prevails with the international CV. In Japan, for example, job hunters still fill out standard forms, available at Japanese book shops. England has a suggested CV form, which is more like the American resume than not.

- If you're applying in a non-English speaking country, have your CV translated into the appropriate foreign language. Send both the English and the native-language version.

- Unless it's untrue, mention in the personal section that you have excellent health.

✔ Suggest by appropriate hobbies and personal interests that you'll easily adapt to an overseas environment.

✔ Handwrite the cover letter that goes with your CV — Europeans use handwriting analysis as a screening device. If your handwriting is iffy, enclose a word-processed version as well.

In addition, make sure that your cover letter shows a sincere desire to be in the country of choice.

Portfolio Format

Samples of your work, gathered in a portfolio, have long been valuable to fields such as design, graphics, photography, architecture, advertising, public relations, and education. Often the portfolios are delivered as part of the job interview, but some highly motivated job seekers include a brief portfolio when sending their resumes.

Even though recruiters say that they prefer less paper, the portfolio format is beginning to gain acceptance over the traditional resume format in other fields as well. The reason is jungle warfare in the job market: Portfolios are a way to prove by the quality of your work that you're right for a specific position.

In designing your portfolio, when you summarize your key points for your resume, include samples that demonstrate each: printed material listing you as the leader of seminars and workshops, performance reviews, easily understandable examples of problem solving and competencies, and work samples. Include praise from employers, people who reported to you, and customers. Make at least two copies of your portfolio in case potential employers decide to hold on to your samples or fail to return them.

Your portfolio should document the skills that you want to apply on the job, so begin by identifying those skills; then determine what would prove your claims.

World Wide Web Format

Sorry, I can't offer a template for preparing World Wide Web pages containing your resume, but I can offer several observations. Until recently, recruiters often did not bother to search online for resumes because it was a lot of work sifting through all the postings. Now, as noted in Chapter 1, sophisticated new search engines seek out specific occupational fields. Most Internet access providers and the commercial online services, such as American Online, CompuServe, and Prodigy, offer free Web pages where you can stash a resume.

Web page wisdom

If you decide to create a Web page, here are some tips:

- Assume that an employer will look for clues to your personality throughout your entire Web page, not just in the resume section. Humor, cartoons? Include funny stuff only when your selection reflects favorably upon you as a quality person. Keep all areas of your page simple and professional.

- Two or three links to other Web resources are plenty, unless you have a reason for more. Linking Web pages merely to show that you know how to do it is amateurish.

- If you send samples of your work that are not protected by copyright or patent flying across the Internet, you may not be able to reclaim the work as your own.

- Posting multiple online resumes can backfire. Suppose you post three different resumes in an attempt to position yourself for three different but related fields, such as CMA (certified management accountant), internal auditor, and CPA (certified public auditor). Even when all three skill packages are legitimate, an inquiring employer may mouse around the Internet and see unfocused-you as three different people. Don't confuse employers by having multiple personalities. Companies more often seek specialists, not generalists.

- During an active job search, remember to check your Web page resume every day to make sure that everything is up and running.

If you can't create your own WebRez (World Wide Web resume), you can have it done for under $50. Ask at computer stores for a Webmaster who can handle the details for you, or inquire at Online Career Center (http://www.occ.com) for a referral.

All the career sites on the World Wide Web give you instructions on how to post your resume after it's completed. Add your e-mail address to the contact information on a paper resume, as well as an address for your Web page resume. (An e-mail address and a Web address are two different things.) People of all ages (particularly new college graduates) are referring employers to URLs (*uniform resource locators* — fancy lingo for a World Wide Web address).

Tip to seasoned aces: Mature people get a youthful-image makeover by using e-mail and the Web and citing those addresses on paper resumes.

Choosing What Works for You

The big closing question to ask yourself when you have settled on a format is *Does this format maximize my qualifications for the job I want?*

If the format you've chosen doesn't promote your top qualifications, take another look at the choices in this chapter and select a format where you can shine.

Chapter 3

Contents Make the KickButt Difference

Deciding what information to put into your resume isn't difficult if you remember the basic purpose: You must show that you can and will provide benefits to an employer. A small lad whom author Robert Fulghum met understood that principle very well. Fulghum wrote about him in *All I Really Need to Know I Learned in Kindergarten (Villard Books, 1988).* The boy rapped on Fulghum's door and handed him this note: *My name is Donnie. I will rake your leaves. $1 a yard. I am deaf. You can write to me. I read. I rake good.*

Regardless of how many sophisticated bells and whistles you add, the content of your resume must tell employers just how well you will rake their leaves.

The Parts of Your Resume

To make your contents easy to access, you organize the facts about you into various categories. Essential parts that make up a resume are

- ✔ Contact information
- ✔ Objective or summary statement
- ✔ Education and training
- ✔ Experience
- ✔ Skills
- ✔ Activities

✔ Organizations

✔ Honors and awards

Other sections that may be included on a resume are

✔ Licenses, work samples

✔ Testimonials

To increase the likelihood that your resume will position you for an interview, take the time to understand the purpose of the different resume parts.

Contact Information

No matter which format you choose, place your name first on your resume, followed by contact information. If your name is not first, a job computer may mistake *Excellent Sales Representative* for your name and file you away as Mr. Representative. Often a name is displayed in slightly larger type and in boldface.

Mailing address. Give a street name with the unit number, city, state, and zip code. If you're a college student or member of the military who will be returning home, give both addresses — *Current Address* and *Permanent Address.*

Valid telephone number. Use a personal number, including the area code, where you can be reached or where the RezReader can leave a message. Do not allow children to answer this line. Do not record a clever message — play it straight. If you must share a telephone with kids, emphasize the need for them to answer the phone professionally and keep their calls short.

Other contact media. Use any or all of the following if available to you: e-mail address, pager number, telephone answering service number, Web page address, or fax number. All cyberspace addresses should appear on separate lines, or be widely spaced on the same line by ample white space. Otherwise, computers may confuse them with street addresses and telephone numbers.

Company resources. Should you ever use your employer's fax number, e-mail address, or letterhead? Many employers see an employee's use of company resources to find another job as small-time theft.

Is it okay to list your work telephone number? In a decade when employers are tossing workers out without remorse, it's a tough world and you need speedy communications. The practical answer is yes, list your work number — if you have a direct line and voice mail or a pager. To show that you are an ethical person, limit calls to a couple of minutes — just long enough to arrange a meeting or an evening callback.

When a company is downsizing, it is expected to provide resource support for outplacement. Contract employment is another exception: When you are ending the project for which you were hired, your employer may encourage you to use company resources. Indicate permission to use them in your resume's cover letter — *The project for which I was hired is finishing ahead of schedule; my grateful employer is cooperating in my new search.*

Hooks: Objective or Summary?

Your KickButt resume needs a hook to grab the RezReader's attention. The hook follows your name and contact information and is expressed as a job objective or as a skills summary — or some combination of the two.

A job objective can look like this:

> **Objective:** Assistant to Executive

A skills summary can look like this:

> **Summary:** More than 14 years of progressively responsible office support experience, including superior computer skills, with an earned reputation for priority-setting and teamwork.

Or a job objective can be linked to a skills summary:

> **Objective:** Assistant to Executive, to keep operations under firm control, using computer skills, contemporary office procedures, and pleasant manner with people.

However fashioned, the hook tells the RezReader what you want to do and/or what you are qualified to do.

Debate rages among career pros over the topic of objective versus summary.

- ✔ Objective backers say RezReaders don't want to slog through a document, trying to guess the type of position you want and how you'd fit into the organization — a serious consideration when they have to hand-sort big stacks of resumes.

- ✔ Summary advocates argue that a thumbnail sketch of your skills allows you to be evaluated for jobs you haven't identified in your job objective — a serious consideration in this new age of computerized resume database searches.

A quick rule of thumb taken from a sampling of six recruiters, recently reported in *Job Choices* magazine, is this: "Objective statement is essential for recent graduates, summary statement for seasoned professionals."

On balance, I agree with the six recruiters: An objective may be a self-defeating force for seasoned aces with well-established career paths, whose insistence on a particular job objective may be seen as rigid, and for those whose resumes will be stored in electronic databases. But an objective is nearly essential for job seekers who are short on experience or do not have a clear idea of what they'd like to do, but know the general direction.

What you really need on your resume is *focus,* whether you style it as a job objective or as a summary. Here are specific points for each type of resume opener.

The job objective statement

Weigh these considerations when deciding how to help readers visualize what you could do in the future for them.

When to use an objective

Use a job objective when

- You are a new graduate, or a career changer exiting the military, the clergy, teaching, or full-time homemaking. A job objective says what you are looking for.
- You have a greatly diversified background that may perplex some employers.
- You know the job being offered; make that job title your job objective.

Advantages of an objective

Most studies show that employers prefer objectives for quick identification purposes. They like to see the name of their job openings and/or companies at the top of a resume. Because you cite those achievements that support your objective and forget random experiences, the finished product (when done well) shows that you and the desired job are a well-matched pair.

Disadvantages of an objective

Do you have the time to write a resume for each position (or career field) to which you apply? A narrow job objective may keep you from being considered by the same employer for other positions. And if the objective is too broadly focused, it becomes a meaningless statement.

The skills summary

A summary statement (see Chapter 8) announces who you are and identifies your strengths. Take a look at what follows.

When to use a summary

Use a summary statement when

- ✔ You are a person with widely applicable skills. Recruiters especially like a skills summary atop a reverse chronological resume because it lets them creatively consider you for countless jobs that you may not know exist. The skills summary gives recruiters greater latitude to consider you for more than one position.

- ✔ You are in a career field with pathways to multiple occupations or industries (an administrative assistant, for example).

- ✔ You know that your resume is headed to an electronic database — or, more likely, you do not know whether humans or computers will screen your resume — and you want to be considered for multiple jobs.

Advantages of a summary

A summary can be more appropriate to status — senior executives, in particular, can let their records speak for them. Recruiters believe that what you're prepared to do next should be pretty evident from what you've already done. Another argument is premised on psychology: Employers are not known for being overly concerned with what you want *from* them until they are sure of what you can do *for* them.

Disadvantages of a summary

A summary does not explicitly say what you want and why the employer would want you. The technique of specifying a job objective in a cover letter attached to a skills-summary resume is common; the problems arise when the cover letter is inadvertently separated from the resume or the resume is passed out alone, as at a job fair. Furthermore, the fact that a skills summary resume leaves many doors open is a two-edged sword: Your accomplishments do not thrust you toward a specific target, so you may be abandoning a success strategy that has been proven again and again.

A summary can be stated in paragraph form or in four to six bulleted quick-hits, such as:

- Recruited and trained more than 300 people
- Installed robotics, standardizing product, reducing retraining cost by 16%
- Slashed initial training costs from $800,00 to $650,000 within one year
- Created dynamic training culture to support the introduction of a new product

What's first — education or experience?

The general rule in resume writing is to lead with your most qualifying factor.

With certain exceptions (such as law, where your choice of alma mater can dog you throughout life), lead off with experience when you've been in the work force for at least three years. When you're loaded with experience but low on credentials, list your school days at the end — and perhaps even omit them entirely if you didn't graduate.

Young people just out of school usually start with education, but if you've worked throughout school or have relevant prior work history, start with experience. Remember, begin with your most qualifying factor for the job you want.

Young readers, if your research shows that a prospective employer wants education and experience, provide a summary linking them together as interdependent. For example, explain how your education was part of your professional experience, or how your experience was an education itself. Following this consolidation, create a heading under which you can merge both sections — such as *Professional Preparation* or *Education, Training, and Employment.*

Education

List your highest degree first — type of degree, major, college name, and date awarded.

- ✔ New graduates give far more detail on course work than do seasoned aces who've held at least one job for one year or more.
- ✔ Omit high school if you have a college degree.
- ✔ If you have a vocational-technical school certificate or diploma that required less than a year to obtain, list your high school as well.

- ✔ Note continuing education, including seminars related to your work.

Experience

Describe — with quantified achievements — your present and previous positions in reverse chronological order. Include dates of employment, company names and locations, and specific job titles. Show progression and promotions within an organization, especially if you have been with one employer for eons.

Consider using more than one Experience heading. Try headings such as "Accounting and Finance-Related Experience," "General Business Experience," and "Healthcare and Administration Experience." This is yet one more way of reinforcing your suitability for the job you seek.

Some resume formats use a more rigid approach than others, allowing little leeway as you fill in the blanks. Most formats, however, leave all kinds of room for stacking your blocks to do you the most good.

Skills

Skills today are the heart and soul of job-finding and, as such, encompass a variety of experiences. These are skills:

Collaborating, editing, fund-raising, extrapolating, interviewing, logical thinking, managing, navigating (Internet), researching, systematizing, teaching

And these are skills:

Administering social programs, analyzing insurance facts, advising homeless people, allocating forestry resources, budgeting in financial industry, desktop publishing, coordinating association events, designing home furnishing ads, marine expedition problem-solving, writing police reports

And these are also skills:

Dependable sense of humor, commitment, leadership, persistence, crisis-resilient, responsible, mature judgment, adaptable, quick-learning, results-driven

And these are still more skills:

> Brochures, UNIX, five years, 100% quota, telemarketing, promotions, senior management, spreadsheet, baccalaureate of science, MBA, Big Six accounting firms

Naming skills as a basic element of resumes may surprise you. I include them here because they have taken on new importance and the skills concept has changed in the past decade. Once, we thought of skills in the classic meaning of general and industry-specific abilities. That notion has expanded to include personal characteristics, as well as past employers, special knowledge, achievements, and products.

As the term is used in job searching today, skill is any identifiable ability or fact that employers value and will pay for.

That means that "five years" is a skill, the same as word processing — employers pay for experience.

Where do skills belong on your resume? Everywhere. Season every statement with skills, if you can. Skills are indispensable. Whether you use a traditional paper resume or a KeyWord electronic resume, you must name your skills or be left behind.

What's the best way to name your skills? See Chapter 12 for an inexpensive booklet on the topic directed at career-changes. Another skills defining resource is a popular card-sorting exercise, Motivated Skills Card Sort Kit, available for $12 from Career Research & Testing in San Jose, California (408-559-4945). Or if you're up for $100 software, the best program I've seen to help uncover all your skills is *Jumpstart* from Up Software in San Francisco (800-959-8208). Available for both PCs and Macs, *Jumpstart* also has a resume-creating section that makes customizing by skills a snap.

Activities

Activities are anything from hobbies and sports to campus extracurricular participation. The trick is to analyze how each activity is relevant to the target job, discussing skills or knowledge developed and listing all achievements. Make sure that this section doesn't become meaningless filler.

In addition, be sure that you don't note potentially controversial activities: Stating that you're a moose hunter will not endear you to RezReading animal lovers. If you've been able to research the RezReader and have found that you two have a common interest, that interest is worth listing on the resume so it can become an icebreaker topic in an interview.

Organizations

Give yourself even more credentials with professional and civic affiliations. Mention all important offices held. Relate these affiliations to your reader in terms of marketable skills, knowledge, and achievements. A high profile in the community is particularly important for sales jobs.

Just as you should be careful about which activities you identify, so too should you be sensitive to booby traps in organization memberships.

- ✔ Listing too many organizations may make the RezReader wonder when you'd have time to do the job.

- ✔ Noting that you belong to one minority group organization may work in your favor, but reporting your membership in five minority group organizations may raise red flags. The RezReader may worry that you're a trouble-making activist who's willing to exhibit poor work performance and unacceptable behavior in order to create a public issue if you're due to get fired.

- ✔ And, of course, you know better than to list your membership in religious or political organizations (unless you're applying for a job that requires such membership). They don't apply to your ability to do the job, and some RezReaders may use them to keep you oput of the hunt.

Honors and Awards

List most of the achievements for which you were recognized. If the achievement had zero to do with work or does not show you in a professional light, don't take up white space with it; you probably would not, for example, list a Chili Cook-Off Winner award.

Testimonials

After you've cited an achievement, you can follow up with a short, flattering quote from your boss or a client:

- (From an information systems technician): *Bob Boss said he was "ecstatic" that I cut Internet access costs by 50%.*

- (From a sales rep at a supercopy shop): *Expanded the SoapSuds account by 15%. How? By contacting not the office manager but the chief financial officer and offering to remove* signature authority of 250 terminated employees. "Jennifer Robertson's resourcefulness in getting inside SoapSuds after others had tried for months is truly impressive," said Barbara Boss, my direct supervisor.

Testimonials work, or advertisers wouldn't use them. Be sure to check with your source before adding the quote to your resume, however. That way, there'll be no surprises.

Licenses and Samples of Your Work

If you are in the legal, certified accounting, professional engineering, or medical profession, you need to add to your resume the appropriate license, certifications, and other identifications required for the position. For a professional resume or CV, you may also need to list descriptions or titles of specific work you have done, or include samples of your work along with your resume. If you're asked to include samples of your work, be selective about what you send. Make sure your samples have no obvious flaws or errors.

Start Fresh, Win Big

With more people fighting for fewer good jobs, you know you can't simply add the latest job description and recirculate the same old resume with updated data. You've got to convince an employer that you will rake their leaves extremely well.

Kick serious butt by focusing on your best content and presenting it forcefully. Because you have very few words to work with, choose precisely the correct words; the next chapter takes you to the word desk. Don't rush the construction of your resume: If you build it (right), the interview will come.

Chapter 4
It's All in the Words

In This Chapter

▶ GoodWords: action verbs that sell you
▶ KeyWords: powerful nouns that sell you
▶ Resume grammar: simple rules that sell you

*W*ords: How powerful they are. It doesn't take many to change the world: The Lord's prayer has 66 words; Lincoln's Gettysburg address numbers just 286 words; and the U.S. Declaration of Independence contains but 1,322 words.

Winston Churchill needed only two words to bind Russia to the *Iron Curtain*. A brief four words memorialized Martin Luther King's vision: *I have a dream.* And in a single sentence, John F. Kennedy set the challenge for a generation: *Ask not what your country can do for you, but what you can do for your country.*

Words are powerful — big words, like *motherland* and *environmentalism,* and small words, like *peace* and *war*, or *dawn, family, hope, love,* and *home.*

Words are pegs to hang your qualifications on. Words are the power that lifts you above the faceless crowd and sets you in Fortune's way. The right words can change your life.

Now begin your hunt for the right words to build a KickButt resume. This chapter shows you how to use *GoodWords,* or action verbs, and *KeyWords,* or nouns, with resume grammar made simple.

GoodWords — used on paper resumes — are action verbs describing your strengths: *improve, upgrade, schedule.* **KeyWords** — used on electronic resumes — are usually nouns demonstrating essential skills: *technology transfers, Ph.D. organic chemistry, multinational marketing.* A smattering of both can make your resume stand up and sing.

GoodWords Can Bring Good News

Resume advisers always urge you to use power-play verbs to communicate your abilities and accomplishments. The action verbs work great on paper resumes, although they're not so great on electronic resumes which tend to scan for nouns. On paper, a punch-zip delivery keeps these achievement-oriented verbs campaigning for you. Try not to use the same word twice on your resume — the thesaurus in a word-processing program can give you more possibilities. The important thing is to choose words of substance and power that zero in on your abilities and achievements.

Take a look at the GoodWords that follow and see which work for you:

GoodWords for administration and management

advised	influenced	prioritized
approved	inspired	processed
authorized	installed	promoted
chaired	instituted	recommended
consolidated	instructed	redirected
counseled	integrated	referred
delegated	launched	reorganized
determined	lectured	represented
developed	listened	responded
diagnosed	managed	reviewed
directed	mediated	routed
disseminated	mentored	sponsored
enforced	moderated	streamlined
ensured	monitored	strengthened
examined	motivated	supervised
explained	negotiated	taught
governed	originated	trained
guided	oversaw	validated
headed	pioneered	
initiated	presided	

GoodWords for communications and creativity

acted	edited	proofread
addressed	enabled	publicized
arranged	facilitated	published
assessed	fashioned	realized
authored	formulated	reconciled
briefed	influenced	recruited
built	initiated	rectified
clarified	interpreted	remodeled
composed	interviewed	reported
conducted	introduced	revitalized
constructed	invented	scheduled
corresponded	launched	screened
costumed	lectured	shaped
created	modernized	stimulated
critiqued	performed	summarized
demonstrated	planned	taught
designed	presented	trained
developed	produced	translated
directed	projected	wrote

GoodWords for sales and persuasion

arbitrated	established	influenced
catalogued	expedited	inspired
centralized	familiarized	installed
consulted	identified	integrated
dissuaded	implemented	interpreted
documented	improved	investigated
educated	increased	judged

launched

lectured

led

liaised

maintained

manipulated

marketed

mediated

moderated

negotiated

obtained

ordered

performed

planned

processed

produced

promoted

proposed

publicized

purchased

realized

recruited

reduced

reported

researched

resolved

restored

reviewed

routed

saved

served

set goals

sold

solved

stimulated

summarized

surveyed

translated

GoodWords for technical ability

analyzed

broadened

charted

classified

communicated

compiled

computed

conceived

conducted

coordinated

designed

detected

developed

devised

drafted

edited

educated

eliminated

excelled

expanded

expedited

fabricated

facilitated

forecast

formed

generated

improved

increased

inspected

installed

instituted

integrated

interfaced

launched

lectured

maintained

marketed

mastered

modified

molded

operated

packaged

pioneered

prepared

processed

programmed

published

reconstructed

reduced

researched

restored

revamped

streamlined

supplemented

surveyed

systematized

trained

upgraded

wrote

GoodWords for office support

adhered

administered

allocated

applied

appropriated

assisted

assured

attained

awarded

balanced

budgeted

built

charted

completed

contributed

coordinated

cut

defined

determined

dispensed

distributed

documented

drafted

enacted

enlarged

evaluated

examined

executed

followed up

formalized

formulated

hired

identified

implemented

improved

installed

instituted

justified

liaised

maintained

managed

operated

ordered

organized

packaged

planned

prepared

prescribed

processed

provided

recorded

repaired

reshaped

resolved

scheduled

screened

secured

solved

started

GoodWords for teaching

acquainted	designed	influenced
adapted	developed	informed
advised	directed	initiated
answered	dispensed	innovated
apprised	distributed	installed
augmented	educated	instituted
briefed	effected	instructed
built	empowered	integrated
certified	enabled	lectured
chaired	enacted	listened
charted	enlarged	originated
clarified	expanded	persuaded
coached	facilitated	presented
collaborated	fomented	responded
communicated	formulated	revolutionized
conducted	generated	set goals
coordinated	grouped	stimulated
delegated	guided	summarized
delivered	harmonized	trained
demonstrated	implemented	translated

GoodWords for research and analysis

administered	augmented	composed
amplified	balanced	concentrated
analyzed	calculated	conducted
applied	charted	constructed
articulated	collected	consulted
assessed	compared	critiqued
audited	compiled	detected

determined	found	pinpointed
discovered	generated	planned
documented	grouped	prepared
drafted	identified	processed
edited	integrated	proofread
evaluated	interpreted	researched
examined	interviewed	reviewed
exhibited	invented	riveted
experimented	investigated	screened
explored	located	summarized
extracted	measured	surveyed
focused	obtained	systematized
forecast	organized	unearthed

GoodWords for helping and caregiving

advanced	counseled	mentored
advised	comforted	ministered
aided	consulted	negotiated
arbitrated	demonstrated	nourished
assisted	diagnosed	nursed
attended	encouraged	nurtured
augmented	expedited	obliged
balanced	facilitated	optimized
backed	familiarized	promoted
braced	fostered	provided
boosted	furthered	reassured
clarified	guided	reclaimed
collaborated	helped	rectified
consoled	instilled	redeemed
contributed	liaised	reeducated

referred	served	streamlined
reformed	settled	translated
rehabilitated	supported	treated
repaired	supplied	tutored
represented	stabilized	unified

GoodWords for financial management

adjusted	eliminated	reported
administered	economized	researched
allocated	exceeded	reshaped
analyzed	financed	retailed
appraised	forecast	saved
audited	funded	shopped
balanced	gained	secured
bought	generated	sold
budgeted	increased	solicited
calculated	invested	sourced
computed	maintained	specified
conciliated	managed	supplemented
cut	marketed	systematized
decreased	merchandised	tested
developed	planned	tripled
dispensed	projected	underwrote
disbursed	purchased	upgraded
distributed	quadrupled	upsized
doubled	reconciled	vended
downsized	reduced	

GoodWords for many skills

accomplished	evaluated	overhauled
achieved	executed	performed
adapted	facilitated	prioritized
adhered	forecast	promoted
allocated	founded	proposed
appraised	governed	reconciled
arbitrated	guided	rectified
arranged	illustrated	remodeled
articulated	improved	repaired
assured	increased	reshaped
augmented	initiated	retrieved
collected	integrated	solved
communicated	interpreted	stimulated
composed	invented	streamlined
conceptualized	launched	strengthened
conserved	led	trained
contributed	navigated	upgraded
coordinated	optimized	validated
demonstrated	organized	won
dispensed	originated	

KeyWords: Key to Electronic Resumes

"Keywords are what employers search for when trying to fill a position," explains James M. Lemke, manager of employment and human resources information at the University of California, Los Angeles.

KeyWords describe the skills or qualifications needed in the person filling the position. Typically, KeyWords are nouns — *counselor* rather than *counseled*. Substitute *management* for *managed*. Nouns are used because that's how positions are usually described. Look at the want ads and check out how they're phrased. Occasionally, a verb will slip out, but don't count on it.

Use all the KeyWords that you truthfully can. Job computers search for KeyWords and retrieve only those resumes that contain the KeyWords, which is why the more KeyWord marketing points you present about yourself, the more often you are likely to be resurrected from an electronic database. Interviews based on electronic resumes rarely happen unless you use nouns.

KeyWords carry clout beyond electronic resumes — they work on paper, too. In a KeyWord summary, which may appear at the top of your resume, specify skills, experience, professional affiliations, and education (see Chapter 2). A KeyWord summary paints a jiffy picture of the essence of your qualifications — a snapshot much appreciated by time-short RezReaders.

How can you find KeyWords for your occupation or career field? Study print and Internet recruitment ads. Jot down nouns appearing with some regularity. Become a KeyWord collector by recording new nouns as you discover them. Use the following sampling of KeyWords organized by field to jump-start your collection.

- **Administration:** contract administration, purchasing, delegation, human resources management
- **Construction:** architecture, civil engineering, construction management, estimates
- **Financial:** banking, arbitrage, Eurodollar loan, futures contract
- **Manufacturing:** assembly, ISO 9000/GMP, packaging, production line
- **Computer:** Animator 1, cyber, Pentium, UNIX C++
- **Marketing/sales:** advertising, demographics, diversity marketing, quota
- **Technical/science:** biochemistry, clinical research, environmental statistics
- **Office support:** fax, computer literate, word processing, desktop publishing

If the RezReader has tunnel vision, KeyWords may be the only way for you to grab attention in an electronic screening process. But be warned: You can't just throw KeyWords on your resume because you think they're attention-getters. You can't, for example, add "P.E." behind your name if you are not a professional engineer. Somewhere in your resume you must legitimize any KeyWord you use by showing how you happen to have that skill or experience.

Get a Grip on Grammar

Resume language differs from normal speech in several ways described here. In general, keep the language tight and the tone professional.

- **First-person pronouns (I, we):** Your name is at the top of each resume page, so the RezReader knows it's about *you*. Eliminate first-person pronouns. Also, don't use third-person pronouns (he, she) when referring to yourself — the narrative technique makes you seem pompous.

- **Articles (the, a, an):** Articles crowd sentences and don't clarify meaning. Substitute *retrained staff* for *retrained the staff.*

- **Helping verbs (have, had, may, might):** Helping verbs weaken claims and credibility — implying that your time has passed and portraying you as a job-hunting weakling. Say *managed* instead of *have managed.*

- **"Being" verbs (am, is, are, was, were):** Being verbs suggest a state of existence rather than a state of motion. Try *monitored requisitions* instead of *requisitions were monitored.* The active voice gives a stronger, more confident delivery.

- **Shifts in tense:** Don't switch back and forth between tenses. Another big mistake: Dating a job as though you are still employed (1994 - Present) and then describing it in the past tense.

- **Complex sentences:** Keep your sentences lean and clean — RezReaders won't take time to decipher them. Process this mind stumper:

  Reduced hospital costs by 67% by creating a patient-independence program, where they make their own beds, and as noted by hospital finance department, costs of nails and wood totaled $300 less per patient than work hours of maintenance staff.

  Complex sentences can be eliminated by dividing ideas into sentences of their own and getting rid of extraneous details:

  Reduced hospital costs by 67%. Originated patient independence program that decreased per-patient expense by $300 each.

- **Overwriting:** Use your own voice; don't say *expeditious* when you want to say *swift.*

- **Abbreviations:** Abbreviations are informal and not universal — even when they are career-specific. Use *Internet* instead of *Net.*

  The exception is industry jargon — use it, especially in electronic resumes. It adds to your credibility to be able to correctly and casually use terms common to the industry in which you're seeking employment.

Here's a trick that writers of television commercials use to be sure they give the most information in the fewest words: Set yourself an arbitrary limit of words to express a unit of information. For example, you might allow yourself 25 words to explain one of your former jobs. The 25-word limit almost guarantees that you'll write with robust language.

Another Reason to Choose Your Words Carefully

Who will screen your resume, deciding whether it's dumpster bait or honcho worthy? A college graduate? A high school dropout? You won't have that information most of the time. When your words speak for you, it's important to use words that everyone can understand and that clearly relate to the job at hand.

Chapter 5

Deadweight: Kick It Out!

. . . .

In This Chapter

▶ Dumping dangerous or useless information

▶ Knowing exceptions to the rules

. . . .

Make every resume fact pack a wallop — if it doesn't, kick that excess baggage right off your pages! Just as you would toss out chipped drinking glasses that might cut your lips, dispose of potentially dangerous admissions. Useless statements have to go, too. Save your precious space for the details that sell you.

Getting Down to Fighting Weight

Here are suggestions on unloading spare facts that weaken your claim to target jobs.

Exceptions exist for almost every guideline. When in doubt about whether to include or omit an item, use this litmus test: *If the fact supports your qualifications for the job you want, include it. If it doesn't, snip, snip, snip.*

Salary needs

Slide aside your salary wishes for now. This blooper undercuts your salary negotiating position. Handle money talk in person after your KickButt resume helps land you a job interview. If a salary history is requested in a recruitment advertisement, you may want to address it in your cover letter as negotiable. (See *Cover Letters For Dummies* for an entire chapter devoted to the salary issue.) Don't include salary figures on your resume — period. Never!

Reasons for leaving other jobs

Because good-bye explanations raise negative questions, the resume is the wrong place to explain why you left.

Exception: You were terminated in a downsizing debacle — which means you weren't at fault. See Chapter 11.

Date available for employment

Drop dates related to when you are available for employment, such as "Available June 2, 1997." If you're still looking on April 4, 1998, the RezReader will wonder why no one hired you.

Exception: If you're a graduating senior or leaving military service, it's okay to list the date you'll be available to start work.

References

Don't include references. Print them on a separate sheet of paper matching your resume to hand out only when requested. References are valuable allies and should not be contacted more than is absolutely necessary. Don't add "References available upon request." That's a given.

Unnecessary headings

Omit extraneous headings such as *Resume;* they're deadweight. White space leaves your resume leaner and is a relief to bloodshot eyes, which is what RezReaders get after plowing through 100 or so resumes.

Unexplained time gaps

A Texas recruiter describes gaps in work histories as "black holes of uncertainty." These black holes raise questions in a RezReader's mind: "Why is there a gap — did you serve time for an act of workplace violence? Do you have a serious illness that will skyrocket insurance rates? What?" See Chapter 11 for suggestions about managing gaps.

Weakening qualifiers

After making a strong statement, don't cut it off at the knees. In an education section, for example, do not say, "Dean's List, one year." Say, "Dean's List," period.

Leave personal info for the Personals section of your daily newspaper.

Marital status

If a job involves travel, will the RezReader be more inclined to hire a single person? If a woman is young and married, will the RezReader worry that she'll bail out soon to start a family? Snip this status report.

Age

Age references plant you in the vulnerable zone. Let RezReaders do the figuring based on other listed dates. Make them work for it! See Chapter 10 for help on ways to combat ageism.

Parents' occupations

Rarely should you reveal how Mom and Dad earn a living (especially if you're over 25!). The data isn't dangerous, but it's certainly useless.

Exception: You may want to note it when a parent's occupation explains a puzzling fact on your resume. Suppose that you want a global traveling position and your resume shows that you're unusually well traveled. You may want to note that your parents were in the Foreign Service, if that's the case. It can also be argued, however, that a little mystery doesn't hurt a job seeker. If a RezReader wants to know why you're so cosmopolitan, you can be invited to an interview where you will resolve the mystery.

Children's names and ages

Wait until the company picnic to break out the family tree. If you're a single parent, the RezReader may anticipate absences due to sick kids.

Ethnicity or national origin

If you run into a prejudiced RezReader, statements of ethnicity or national origin may hinder your chances for an interview. Discriminating on the basis of ethnicity or national origin went out of style with the Civil Rights Act of 1964; these issues have no relevance to your suitability for a job. Don't make an issue of them on your resume.

Physical description or photograph

Concerned about charges of discrimination, smart companies don't want to see what you look like. Give your honey the picture.

Exception: If you're a model or an actor, you need to include a photo.

Health

The Americans with Disabilities Act of 1990 directs employers to snip the health question. Even if you're in excellent health, the information is meaningless — no one ever writes "sickly health."

Leisure activities

Some — but certainly not all — RezReaders make the argument that reporting leisure activities amplifies a candidate's profile and that they want to see "what kind of person you are." Maybe so, but as a rule of thumb, don't waste resume space on hobbies.

Exception: Note leisure activities that qualify you for the target position. Or, even when your paid experience qualifies you, you may believe that your leisure activities gild the lily. Does the activity have an inferred relationship to the job you want? Playing chess, for example, is a good hobby for a management consultant where strategizing is important. Green-thumb expertise is magic when applying for a job at a plant nursery.

New KickButt Resume Maxims

Blue pencil in hand, strike out any bits of jetsam and flotsam gunking up your resume. Get in the mood for major resume surgery by glancing at these office guides:

- ✔ It's not only what you write, it's how fast the RezReader can find it.
- ✔ Handling a problem in your history: It takes less space to avoid the problem than to explain it.
- ✔ Never tell them what you don't want known.

Part II
Creating Your
KickButt Resume

The 5th Wave   **By Rich Tennant**

MIKE USES HIS SKILLS WORKING AT A POP-UP CARD COMPANY TO CREATE A MEMORABLE RESUME.

In this part ...

How do you start to build your KickButt resume? You start by identifying your selling points. The worksheets that follow can help. Scribble away on them, and you'll have the material you need to create a ferociously strong resume that nobody backs into a corner.

Chapter 6

Designing Your Dream Job

. . . .

In This Chapter

▶ Focusing on what you want

▶ Focusing on what you do not want

. . . .

*A*ikido is the Japanese word for one of the more sophisticated disciplines in martial arts. *Ai* means harmony or oneness; *ki* is energy or spirit, or spirit of the universe; and *do* means the way or path. A major difference between aikido and other forms of martial arts (such as KickButt moves) is that aikido is completely defensive.

In this Aikido-style assessment, you defend yourself against those horrific episodes in your work history that you never want to visit again, and you bring into sharp relief the experiences that revealed to you what working happiness is.

The subjects accentuated include positive reasons why you left previous jobs, beneficial lessons learned in previous jobs, the components that you really want in a job, the skills and responsibilities that you enjoy using well, and those that you would like to use and improve in future jobs.

This worksheet offers the opportunity to identify factors you wish to avoid in a job and lets you examine which of your transferable skills from leisure activities puts roses in your bouquet of fulfilling activities. Doing this will help you identify prospective jobs that are likely to pay off well for you and your employer — jobs that you can really sell yourself for in your resume.

Make copies of this worksheet for each job that you want to review. Take a step toward losing a desperate I-need-any-job panic — find that pencil the cat hid under the sofa and sharpen it. Go to work on the worksheet that follows.

Aikido-Style Worksheet

Reasons for Leaving Job

Employer: _____ From: _____ (Year) To: _____ (Year)

What did you most like about your job here and why did you apply for it in the first place? _____

_____

_____

_____

What did you most dislike about your job here? _____

_____

_____

_____

Why did you choose to leave (pay? title? no promotion? unfulfilling?)? _____

_____

_____

_____

Areas of Highest Performance

Of the skills you used here, which gave you the most satisfaction
(give example)? Why? _____

_____

_____

_____

Of the duties, which made you feel your best? Why? _____

_____

_____

Which skills and responsibilities would you like to use in your next job? _____

_____

_____

_____

What You Never Want in a Job

Of the skills you used here, which were the least fulfilling? _____

_____

_____

_____

Which tasks did you dread most? Why? _____

_____

_____

_____

Your Most Attractive Attributes

In your leisure activities, which skills have you used that can transfer to your

next job? _____

_____

_____

_____

Don't bother writing a summary of this exercise; its message will be indelible in your mind.

Chapter 7
Working the Worksheets

. . . .

In This Chapter

▶ Sizing up your education and training

▶ Examining your paid skills

▶ Reviewing your unpaid work skills

▶ Translating your hobbies/activities to skills

▶ Assessing your employability skills

. . . .

*R*emember, a KickButt resume is based on the matching of two essential factors:

✔ Company research as a tool to define your suitability for the open position

✔ Meticulous self-assessment — and superb presentation of the assessment

Like Chapter 6, this chapter zeroes in on the second point, self-assessment — this time from the aspect of what an employer would want in you.

You can't present the best of yourself until you have a handle on the goods. Harold W. Ross, founding editor of the urbane and wildly successful *New Yorker* magazine, got that gem of wisdom dead straight when he drolly assessed who he was in the scheme of things.

Ross, a high school dropout and a Colorado miner's son who blew out of the Silver West nearly a century ago to become a famous figure in American journalism and letters, once advised a staff member of the magazine:

"I am not God," he reportedly said. "The realization of this came slowly and hard some years ago, but I have swallowed it by now. I am merely an angel in the Lord's vineyard."

On these pages, you get a chance to show why you, too, are an angel. I assume that you already have labored in the vineyards of career determination and have a fair idea of the kind of job or career field that you want to lay siege to. (If not, back up and pursue the issue of career choice with a counselor or read a relevant book, such as *Joyce Lain Kennedy's Career Book (VGM Career Horizons)* for rookies, or *I Could Do Anything If I Only Knew What It Was* by Barbara Sher (Delacorte Press) for seasoned aces.)

As you flip pages and anticipate the task ahead, I don't want to hear one word of protest about too much rigmarole. The assessment exercises in this and the following chapter give you the design tools you need to craft resumes too good to be ignored. Throw your shoulder into them whether you are a raw rookie or a seasoned professional, executive, manager, or other pooh-bah. After you finish the evaluations, what a job dealmeister you'll be!

Collectively, these worksheets lead to the creation of a personal inventory. My strategy for building a personal inventory is for you to first collect and document your job-qualifying skills. Don't waste time by starting off with an effort to photograph your inner self with words — "I'm intuitive," "I'm sensitive," "I'm insightful." Get to the meat of the matter right away. Too many RezWriters are convinced that they have no marketable skills, no relevant experience, no desirable attributes, and no hirable traits. Discouraged, they give up and just throw a bare outline on paper. Big mistake. Think a lot! Write a lot!

The worksheets that follow are the front-runners of a powerful summary of summaries described in the next chapter. Each worksheet looks at your life in a wide-angle, rear-view mirror and then narrows the focus by suggesting that you target the most useful and vital accomplishments.

Many people lose the resume derby because they merely report where they have worked and enumerate the duties they were assigned. That information alone won't karate the competition.

- ✔ What did you accomplish?
- ✔ What value did you bring to a specific position?
- ✔ What did it matter that you showed up at the office most days?
- ✔ How have you put your degree to work?
- ✔ What good has your education done anyone?

It's the *identification* and *measurement* of *results*, *outcomes*, and *achievements* that make recruiters book you for interviews.

If you still have the pencil that the cat dragged off, begin your inventory of education, paid work skills, unpaid work skills, hobbies and activities translated to skills, and employability skills.

Education and Training Worksheet

Name of institution/program _____

Address _____ Telephone _____

Year(s) attended or graduated _____ Degree/diploma/certificate _____

Overall GPA _____ Major GPA _____ Class rank (if known) _____

Work-relevant study

(Photocopy and complete one worksheet for each relevant course)

Course _____

Knowledge acquired _____

_____

Skills acquired _____

_____

Accomplishments (with concrete examples) _____

_____

Relevant projects/papers; honors _____

_____

KeyWords/GoodWords (see Chapter 4) _____

Quotable remarks by others (names, contact data) _____

_____

_____

Paid Work Worksheet

(Photocopy and complete one worksheet for each job)

Name of employer _____

Postal address, e-mail address, telephone, fax _____

_____

_____

_____

_____

Type of business/career field _____

Job title _____

Dates _____

Direct supervisor's name, contact information (if good reference; otherwise,

note coworkers or sources of good references) _____

_____

_____

_____

_____

Major accomplishments (Promotion? Awards? Business achievements? —
"increased sales by 30 percent" or "saved company 12 percent on office
purchases"? What credit can you claim for creating, implementing, revamping,
designing, saving? Jog your memory by recalling problems faced and action
taken.) _____

_____

_____

Problems faced _____

_____

_____

_____

Action taken _____

_____

_____

_____

_____

Skills acquired _____

_____

_____

_____

Job responsibilities _____

_____

_____

_____

KeyWords/GoodWords _____

_____

_____

_____

Quotable remarks by others (names, contact data) _____

_____

_____

_____

_____

Unpaid Work Worksheet

(Photocopy and complete one worksheet for each relevant unpaid job)

Name of Employer _____

Type of organization _____

Volunteer job title _____

Dates _____

Direct supervisor's name, contact information _____

_____

Major accomplishments (What credit can you claim for creating, implementing, revamping, designing, saving? Jog your memory by recalling problems faced and action taken.) _____

_____

_____

_____

Problems faced _____

Action taken _____

Skills acquired _____

Keywords/GoodWords _____

Quotable remarks by others (names, contact data) _____

_____

_____

_____

Hobbies/Activities-to-Skills Worksheet

(Photocopy and complete one worksheet for each relevant activity)

Name of hobby, organization, club (location) _____

_____

Dates _____

Title/position (officer/member) _____ Elected (yes/no)

Accomplishments _____

_____

_____

_____

Work-related skills acquired _____

_____

_____

Knowledge acquired _____

_____

_____

_____

KeyWords/GoodWords _____

_____

_____

Quotable remarks by others (names, contact data) _____

_____

_____

_____

Employability Skills Worksheet

(Photocopy and complete one worksheet for each relevant course)

Name of company/supervisor _____

Aspects of your work ethic that the employer appreciated _____

_____

Example _____

Facets of your personality that the employer valued _____

_____

Example _____

Name of co-worker/client/industry contact _____

Aspects of your work ethic that the person appreciated _____

_____

_____

Example _____

_____

Facets of your personality that the person valued _____

_____

Example _____

KeyWords/GoodWords _____

_____

Chapter 8

Drafting Summary Statements That Sizzle

*Y*ou say you've filled out forms until your pen's run dry? You say *nuts* to this whole paper parade?

Understandable.

I don't like filling out forms either. I'd be in favor of burning the whole paper shebang, except that torching it would dramatically lower your chances of surviving in a new kind of job market. A job market that, considering ongoing massive job cuts, seems to deserve an allegorical sign on its door:

> *Please the Investors, Punish the Workers.*

I'm not being flip. Powerful business forces are ganging up to put in harm's way not only American workers but job holders throughout the world's advanced economies. You need all the help you can give yourself. If that means becoming more PPP — *proficient* at *packaging* and *presenting* what you have to sell — so be it.

Here's a real day-downer: Of 125 million Americans working today, nearly one fourth are in jeopardy of losing their jobs. This forecast comes from George David, CEO of United Technologies. A corporate chieftain at the helm of American industry, David recently told the National Press Club in Washington:

> *As many as 30 million of these [125 million American workers] will be at*
> *risk: 18 million people in administrative support jobs prone to automation,*
> *10 million in manufacturing jobs susceptible to foreign competition, and*
> *2 million in additional white-collar jobs that medium and large companies,*
> *under the pressure of competition, will learn to live without.*

No more grumbling about being buried in a paper avalanche, okay? Sit up
straight and continue your form-filled, genuine, career moment. After you
compile the data from Chapter 7, sift through it and go back over everything
you've done, circling the items that relate most closely to the job you want.
Hone in on the power-packed information summaries that your resume needs
to lift you out of the masses of unemployed, underemployed, misemployed, and
future nonemployed people.

Why You Need Power Summaries

Power summaries get you to create a muscle statement of *position-related* skills,
achievements, education, and other special qualifications to use primarily for
the opening of your resume. But power summaries provide several other
benefits as well. A quick overview:

- ✔ **Opening statement:** Despite various nuances, a power summary is
  basically a skills summary. It is also called a highlights statement, profile
  section, marketing summary, objective/summary, KeyWord summary,
  KeyWord profile, professional history capsule, and qualifications summary.

  The summary contains the three to five best skills (sales points) that
  support your job aspiration. The exception to this definition of the
  summary is in KeyWord resumes (see Chapter 2) — use all relevant skills
  when you characterize yourself with one-phrase nouns rather than full
  sentences. *Important: The data need not be proven with examples in this
  section; it can stand alone for now.* You are saying, "Here's who I am, and
  here's what I can do for you." The tease is to read on for proof of what the
  opening says.

- ✔ **Summary page:** A power summary can be expanded to an entire summary
  page, which you place atop a reverse chronological resume (in effect
  turning your reverse chronological resume into a hybrid resume format, as
  discussed in Chapter 2).

- ✔ **Old successes:** A power summary can revive a fading job achievement.
  Suppose you have an achievement that took place four or five years ago
  and is now needed to qualify you for a job. By amplifying the old achievement in a summary statement (and perhaps choosing a functional format
  for your resume), you don't bury it in a bazaar of your past jobs. When
  crystallized in a focused power summary, the golden oldie achievement
  still works for you.

✔ **Basis for achievement statements:** Power summaries provide the raw material for achievement sections (paragraphs) and brief (one- or two-line) high-voltage statements that you use later in your resume. *Important: Data in achievement statements must be proven by examples, the best of which are quantified. Measure, measure, measure!*

What's the difference between an opening statement and the achievement statements that are used later in your resume? The difference is where you incorporate documentation, or "storytelling," to authenticate what you're saying. Opening statements are credible without examples or results; achievement statements are not credible without examples and results.

So do KickButters ever give examples or results in an opening statement? You can bet your booties they do. And those examples may add to the sell, provided that they aren't merely repeated later on. *Reinforcing themes by revisiting related issues is good,* but rehashing the very same thing on a resume looks like you attended copycat school.

In addition to putting steel in your resume, power summaries provide you with a workout for interviews. When you're asked to describe yourself, you'll be prepared to deliver the message as smoothly as a network news anchor.

A Sampling of Power Summaries

To lend a helping hand, I give you a few examples of power summaries suitable for opening statements.

Human resources manager

Well-rounded experience in all human resource functions. Specialization: Benefits and Labor Relations. Managed HR staff of 200,000-population, unionized city. Reputation for progressive programs attractive to both city and employees.

Marketing account executive

Award-winning marketer with impressive performance record in Internet merchandising. Proficient in international conventions and customs. Attentive to details while focusing on the big picture. Excellent at organizing, tracking, and managing projects. Relates well to customers and co-workers.

Construction manager

General construction-manager experience covers all areas: start-up and financing, site selection, building design, and construction. Hire and train. Properties never litigated. Work ahead of schedules. Rehired several times by same developers.

Junior accountant

Seek opportunity to demonstrate superior accounting skills developed at top-rated Midwestern university where ranked in top 5% of class. GPA 3.8. Dean's List. Class officer. Computer software: Peachtree Accounting, QuickBooks Pro, MYOB Accounting, Windows 95, Word, WordPerfect. Enthusiastic, eager learner. Single. Happy to travel, relocate.

The personal information included in the junior accountant's combination objective/summary statement is provided as an additional plus. Normally, except in international C.V. resumes, you want to avoid listing personal information, and employers in the U.S. cannot require that you include it. "Single. Happy to travel, relocate" is a good addition for jobs not in your city of residence or for jobs that may require frequent travel.

Technical support manager

Well-qualified senior manager with more than 15 years' experience in software industry, 8 of the last 10 with Microsoft. Professional history proves I can cost-effectively manage support systems and supply consulting services for field, regional, and national areas. Directed staff of 12 managers, 40 analysts, overseeing seven-figure profit center.

Communications graduate

Entry opportunity in print or broadcast news. Completing communications degree, with minor in English. Interned as editorial associate in newspaper columnist's office, achieved top performance review; editor of college newspaper; instructor of adult students at writing lab.

Hospitality manager

Superior comprehensive management record. Check me out on profit and cash flow, cost controls, financial reporting of operating figures, food and beverage for restaurant rooms, catering, entertainment booking, golf course, and club house. Developing convention business is my specialty. Use all current accounting software.

Note: The "check me out" this candidate uses matches the strong sell the candidate is trying to convey. A glad-hander is good for the hospitality industry, and she's showing she has what it takes.

Contract specialist

Six years' experience in contract negotiation, promoted from *assistant to processor* to *contract administrator* in first two years. Developed streamlining strategies for JIT contract delivery, beating schedule requirements by two days. Familiar with relevant aspects of finance and law, including budgeting, contract estimation, and contract litigation and legality.

Sifting through Your Data

Turn to each of your worksheets (if you don't have any worksheets, check out Chapter 7) and concentrate on the data that most clearly show how well you qualify for the job — or jobs — that you want.

Use the following forms to transfer data that explain why you are qualified for the position you seek.

Note in the left column of the PreSummary Worksheet what the employer wants in the target job or career field. Get this information from recruitment ads, job descriptions, and occupational literature.

In the right column, drawing the information from your worksheets, jot down how you meet each requirement with a qualification.

When the job calls for specific skills, the employer doesn't necessarily care how or where you obtained the requisite skills in the summary— so the headings in the left column merely say *Skills Required.*

PreSummary Worksheet

The Employer Wants **You Have**

Education and Training Required	Education and Training Skills — Including Achievements
1)	
2)	
3)	
4)	
5)	
Skills Required	Paid Skills — Including Achievements
1)	
2)	
3)	
4)	
5)	

(1 of 2)

PreSummary Worksheet

The Employer Wants ➡ You Have

Skills Required	Unpaid Skills — Including Achievements
1)	
2)	
3)	
4)	
5)	
Skills Required	Hobby/Activity Skills — Including Achievements
1)	
2)	
3)	
4)	
5)	
Skills Required	Employability Skills — Including Achievements
1)	
2)	
3)	
4)	
5)	

(2 of 2)

By contrast, the headings in the right column correspond to the worksheets in Chapter 7; they are noted here as yet another reminder to include your skills from any source — paid or unpaid.

Prepare a Power Worksheet for each target job or career field.

More paperwork! Why aren't you surprised? Move the best material from the PreSummary Worksheet onto your Power Summary worksheet.

Yes, you can write a summary based on your Chapter 7 worksheets and skip the middle step of making a PreSummary worksheet. And maybe you want to do it that way. Others find it easier to use an additional transfer step and also find the PreSummary worksheet a reinforcing action to focus on targeting, targeting, targeting.

Power Summary Worksheet

The Employer Wants	You Have
Employer 1)	Summary 1)
Employer 2)	Summary 2)

Power patterns

Remember, you don't have to prove what you say right there in the opening statement or summary — but you do have to prove it later in your resume, in achievement statements. Here's a collection of write-in forms to start you off. Just fill in the blanks.

After _____ (number of years, provided the number is not too high) years in _____ (your occupation), seek opportunity to use extensive experience and_____ (your favorite skills) as a_____(your target position).

Knowledge of_____(your expertise) and familiarity with_____ (type of product, industry, or clientele). Seek position as _____ (job title) using intensive experience as a _____ (occupation).

Developed new _____ which resulted in increased _____ ; maintained an aggressive _____ program that increased employer's revenues by _____ %. Seeking a position as a _____ (your objective) in an organization needing expertise in _____(your top skills).

A position as a _____ (a job slightly higher in rank than your top employment), specializing in _____ (a skill unique to you).

A (type of) position that needs _____ (list skills and accomplishments). Demonstrated by (list of paid and volunteer responsibilities and successes). Will _____ (an improvement that your prospective employer appreciates).

Offering _____ (your field) skills in _____ (related industry), with ability to solve_____ (one or more problems common in the field), including _____ (your top skills).

Encyclopedic knowledge of _____ (your top skills in technical aspects of position), familiarity with _____(qualifying duties of position), and effective management of_____ (your lesser job-related skills).

Aim for Powerful but True Statements

Confession: As a new college graduate, after having served as a campus reporter for *Mademoiselle* magazine, I wrote my way into a job as a fashion coordinator for a dress manufacturer in St. Louis. It never occurred to me that unfamiliarity with fashion beyond reading a couple of books would be as big a problem as the sales staff thought it was. I was involuntarily out of there in two weeks.

Review your finished summaries the next day. Did you get carried away with fantasy writing? Ask yourself, "Can I live up to this advance billing?" If not, tone it down to reality — that is, your *best reality.* Unfortunately — you smooth writer, you — when you land a job based on hype that you can't back up, you should be ready to renew your job search.

Heed this good advice from California newspaper columnist Thomas J. Morrow:

"Never sell more of yourself than you can later buy back with skill and performance."

Chapter 9

Nailing Down the KickButt Look

● ●

In This Chapter

▶ Creating great-looking paper resumes

▶ Incorporating graphic elements that sell you

▶ Simplifying the visuals for electronic resumes

● ●

*Y*ou don't know where your resume will land. You don't know whether your resume will be initially viewed by human eyes or by computer chips. You don't know who will decide what happens to you as a result of your resume.

But you do know that your resume had better look *better* than good.

It's not logical, but it's true: A paper resume that looks superb is assumed to be superb and will trigger far more readership than will a visually inferior document with average content.

As the competition for good jobs grows fiercer by the year, you can't afford a resume that a RezReader perceives as second-rate and doesn't read further. This chapter offers an overview of do's and don'ts. Check out the sample resumes in Chapters 13 and 14 to see examples of how your resume can look.

Paper Resumes that Keep On Kicking

Although the market is moving away from paper resumes, trees-and-ink remain the dominant resume technology for most people. Here's how to look outstanding on paper and make the first cut in the employment screening process.

Word processing

You need a computer equipped with word-processing software to produce your resume. Typewritten copies are still acceptable, but most people don't type well enough to produce crisp, clean, sparkling copies. If word processing is not yet one of your skills, scout out a word-processing class — you'll need this ability in nearly any job you take. In the meantime, find a friend who will key in your resume. If you have the skill but not the tools, can you use a friend's computer? Rent a computer by the hour at supercopy shops? Use a computer at a school's computer lab? If none of this is possible, take your handwritten resume to a professional office support firm and hire someone to do the production work.

Unemployed people can use computers for free at Private Industry Council (PIC) offices nationwide; ask for PIC locations at public employment service offices.

Printing

Producing your resume on a laser or inkjet printer is today's standard. The old-fashioned dot matrix printers lack the firepower to print resumes that compete in today's job market. If you photocopy a core resume — rather than custom-tailor each resume to the job at hand — make sure that the copies look first-rate. No blurring, stray marks, streaks, or faint letters.

Paper

How good must your paper be? For professional, technical, managerial, and executive jobs, the stock for a paper resume should be quality paper with rag content, perhaps 25 percent, and a watermark (a faint image ingrained in the paper). Small printing firms and specialty-paper mail-order catalogs offer a wide range of choices. Restrict the color of your paper to white or off-white, eggshell, or very pale gray. Print on one side of the sheet only.

The ink on a KickButt resume is evenly distributed across each page, which is best achieved with a smooth paper stock. The image evoked by a high-quality paper is diminished when it looks as though the ink just didn't flow consistently — the print looks alternately dark or faded, and there may be smears or streaks. Linen (textured) paper is impressive, but the ink from a laser printer or photocopier may not move smoothly across a sheet, making your resume hard to read. Try before you buy. If there's the slightest doubt about readability, switch to laid (smooth) paper.

The quality of paper is immaterial when your resume is to be scanned into job computers or spun across the Internet. Hiring managers never see it.

Open spaces

Which style of reading do you prefer: a paper so packed with text that your eyes need a spa treatment before tackling it, or a paper so generous with white space that you *want* to read it? You'd be surprised how many people, hearing that they must not exceed one page, try to cram too much information in too little space.

A ratio of about one quarter white space to text is about right. Line spacing between items is vital. Do not justify the right side of the page — that is, do not try to have the type align down the right side of the page — leave it ragged. Right justification creates awkward white spaces. An overcrowded page almost guarantees that it will not be read by younger RezReaders who grew up in an age of television and *USA Today*–style newspapers. And older RezReaders? Their eyes won't take the wear and tear of too many words crashing in too small a space. White space is the master graphic attention-getter.

Typefaces and fonts

A *typeface* is a family of characters — letters, numbers, and symbols. A *font* is a specific size of typeface, which is generally measured in points (each point $1/72$ of an inch). Helvetica is a typeface; Helvetica 10-point bold, Helvetica 12-point bold, and Helvetica 14-point bold are three different fonts.

The two basic classes of typefaces are *serif* and *sans-serif* (See Figure 9-1). Serif typefaces such as Times Roman have cross-lines at the ends of character strokes and tend to look curved and elegant. *Sans* means *without* in French. Sans-serif typefaces like Helvetica do not have cross-lines and are simple and clean.

Typefaces and their fonts are tricky. Your computer can print a variety of typefaces and fonts — book, italics, bold lettering — and other graphic elements, once available only at printers' shops. Whipping out a fancy-looking

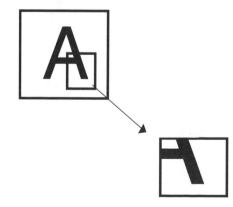

Figure 9-1:
Examples of serif and sans-serif typefaces. Note the cross-lines at the ends of the serif character strokes.

Times Roman

Helvetica

piece of paper has become so easy that some resumes, overweight with a jumble of excess typefaces and fonts, tip over and sink to the bottom of the applicant pile. Showing an enormous lack of judgment by their writers, these design-happy resumes are the paper equivalent of resorting to shouting when your argument is weak. RezReaders go nuts trying to read the stuff.

Here's a technique that advertising pros use to avoid going overboard on design: Tape versions of your resume on a wall and decide which one looks classy and attractive.

Tips on typefaces

Times Roman is a popular serif typeface. Examples:

- ✔ 10-pt. Times Roman book
- ✔ **10-pt. Times Roman bold**
- ✔ *10-pt. Times Roman italics*
- ✔ 12-pt. Times Roman book
- ✔ **12-pt. Times Roman bold**
- ✔ *12-pt. Times Roman italics*
- ✔ 14-pt. Times Roman book
- ✔ **14-pt. Times Roman bold**
- ✔ *14-pt. Times Roman italics*

Helvetica is a popular sans-serif typeface. Examples:

- ✔ 10-pt. Helvetica (basic)
- ✔ **10-pt. Helvetica bold**
- ✔ *10-pt. Helvetica italics*
- ✔ 12-pt. Helvetica book
- ✔ **12-pt. Helvetica bold**
- ✔ *12-pt. Helvetica italics*
- ✔ 14-pt. Helvetica book
- ✔ **14-pt. Helvetica bold**
- ✔ *14-pt. Helvetica italics*

No more than two typefaces should appear on one resume; if you don't have an eye for what looks good, stick to one typeface. Either Times Roman or Helvetica used alone is a fine choice for your resume. But if you want to mix the two typefaces, choose Helvetica for the headings and Times Roman for the text and lesser headings. Why? A serif typeface is considered the more readable in blocks of copy, which is why most newspapers and this book use a serif typeface for the text. Look at the sample resumes in Chapter 14 for ideas on how to mix and match various typefaces.

Many typefaces are akin to each other and not easily distinguishable to the graphics nonprofessional. If you don't have Times Roman, similar typefaces are equally pleasing, such as a proportionally spaced Courier, CG Omega, Garamond, and New Century Schoolbook.

If you don't have Helvetica, comparable typefaces include Futura, Letter Gothic, Optima, and Univers.

Font sizes

Type is measured in points, with 72 points equalling one inch. A standard font size is usually 10 points with the same amount of *leading* (space) between the lines. *Kerning* is the space between characters; employ it to condense or spread a heading or line of text. Most word-processing programs let you adjust the kerning of individual letters. If you don't know how, accept the program's default kerning.

Paying attention to the spacing of your resume contributes much to its readability. Printing the RezWriter's name in small capital letters can be pleasing. Using larger type for headings (12 or 14 pt) or bold face can give necessary prominence. Use italics sparingly — you don't want to overdo emphasis, and italicized words lose readability in blocks of text. Most job computers cannot read italics.

Design structure

Your name and contact information can be flush left, centered, or flush right. Look at examples in Chapter 14.

Some RezReaders suggest that you type your name flush- right because they thumb through the right-hand corner of resume stacks.

Aim for a tasteful amount of capitalization and bold lettering for emphasis. Unless you're willing to risk a train wreck of blurred text, omit underlining. On names, for example, **F**red **F**igler may become **E**red **E**igler.

Important information jumps in the RezReader's face when set off by bullets, asterisks, and dashes.

Typos and spelling errors are unacceptable. They are seen as carelessness or lack of professionalism. It is far better that I have a spelling mistake in this book than you have one in your resume. In the tens of thousands of resumes sent to me for review as a columnist (a service I do not offer, by the way), spelling has at times been creative. One man claimed to be *precedent* of his company. Do you think he was a good one? Use your computer's spell-checker and read your finished resume carefully.

Do not staple together a two-or three-page resume or put it in a folder or plastic insert. The resume may be photocopied and distributed, or it may be scanned into a database. To minimize the risk of a page becoming an orphan, put a simple header atop each page after the first: Your name and page number. In a multiple page resume, it's a good idea to indicate how many pages there are, as in page 1 of 2, in case the pages get separated. You can also put the page number at the bottom.

Your KickButt Resume Is Moving Right Along

How much time do you think you have invested in your resume project so far — several days? Is your time well invested? You be the judge! A large California corporation advertised for a sales representative to sell a technical product to other businesses. More than 600 people applied for the position, of whom 10 were selected for interviews. The remaining 590 applicants never made the first cut. Their resumes didn't give them high-priority status as top candidates.

Take the time to make sure your resume is as strong as it can be to attract the employer who's right for you. The resume samples later in this book can give you a good idea of the variety of clean-cut, appealing resume designs you can adopt.

Part III
Solving Specific
Resume Stumpers

The 5th Wave — By Rich Tennant

©RICHTENNANT

"ACCORDING TO THIS RESUME YOU'VE DONE A LOT OF JOB-HOPPING."

In this part ...

Age and experience — the wrong kind — can turn your resume into an obit. Responsibly upgrade any factor that RezReaders may perceive as negative. Lying is foolish, but positioning the issue in the best possible light can warm interview chairs.

Chapter 10

Spin Control against Deadly Perceptions

. . . .

In This Chapter

▶ Squaring off on the overqualified objection

▶ Battling ageism

▶ Stretching too little experience

▶ Coping with new-graduate challenges

▶ Standing tall as a reentering woman

. . . .

Spin control means that when you can't change the facts of your experience or age, you change their presentation.

Sorry, we found someone more qualified (read younger)

Sorry, you're overqualified

Sorry, you have too little experience

Sorry, you have no experience

Sorry, you have no recent experience

All of these common rejection statements call for spin control, or putting the best face on a perception.

You can't strip away 20 years. Nor can you wipe away a substantial background that causes you to be ignored because you're "overqualified."

You can't beef up experience you don't have. Nor can you, as a new graduate, magically add work experience to your resume if you "forgot" to hold a student job or to do the college internship or co-op job that your parents and counselors nagged you to death about.

Or perhaps you don't want to lose your place in the corporate line because, as a mom, you chose to stay home with the kids and infuse them with family values.

Spin control to the rescue!

This chapter spotlights major resume components that need spin control to ward off an early burial for your resume. These components are the quintessential and potentially disabling perceptions that stem from your age, old or young; the abundance of your experience; and the experience that seemingly isn't there when you start out or return to the job market.

If you're tempted to skip over this chapter, which deals with reshaping perceptions, you have my permission — if you're no older than 35 and have five years' experience that precisely matches the requirements for a job that you want. Otherwise, sit down, read up, and fight on!

Too Much Experience

Leading off the lineup of resume stumpers is a focus on the shady side of the four-letter word that's 10-letters long: *experience.*

The E-word's assignment to pejorative status is justified. Not only is inappropriate experience — too much or too little — often the real reason you're turned down, but it's also too frequently a cover story for villainous rejections really based on any factor from bias to bad breath.

Too many qualifications or ageism?

A reader of my newspaper column, "Careers," who is rounding the 50s curve, writes that his qualifications for a training position are superior but too ample. He explains:

> *Preoccupation with age seems to be the pattern. I'm rarely called for an interview; when I call after sending a resume in response to an ad or a networking contact, I'm told I'm too experienced for the position — "You seem to be overqualified." How can I keep my resume from looking like lavender and old lace?*

Ageism often is the subtext in the *overqualified* objection. Deal with it by limiting your work history to the most recent positions you've held that target the job opening. To avoid seeming too old or too highly paid, limit your related experience to about 15 years for a managerial job and to about 10 years for a technician job. Concerns about how you moved up so fast will arise if you only go back 10 years for a managerial job, but 10 years is believable for a technical job.

What about all your other experience? Leave it in your memory banks. Or if you believe that the older work history adds to your value as a candidate, you can describe it under a heading of **Other Experience** and briefly present it without dates. Figure 10-1 shows an example of a resume that shows recent experience only.

RECENT EXPERIENCE ONLY

Work Experience.

FEIN AND SONS -- Operates continuously in Long Beach. **Sole Proprietor, Broker.**
Real estate brokerage, development, asset management and consulting. In-house brokerage company, specializing in eight- and nine-figure acquisitions, shopping centers, and commercial space, obtaining entitlements and economic analysis. Personal volume: over $100 million.

SONNHAARD INC. -- Solana Beach. 1993-1995. **Marketing Manager.**
Real estate development corporation. Primary project: Le Chateau Village, a French-theme 100-lot residential development in Del Mar. Sourced architect, designers, and contractors. Limited liability company built 60 upscale custom homes by architect Jacques Donnaeu of Toulouse. Supervised 10 sales representatives. Sales gross exceeded $40 million, selling 58 homes ahead of project schedule by six months.

WEST COAST ASSOCIATION -- Los Angeles. 1979-1993. **Executive Vice President.**
International trade association with 190 firms holding annual fairs, from 25 states and all of Canada, including two theme amusement parks. 15 affiliated breed organizations and 300 service members who provide goods and services to members. Annual convention attended by over 2,000 executives. Acted as legislative advocate for California district and county fairs, nine of which have horse racing and pari-mutuel wagering. Increased membership by 200%, administering seven-figure budget, with staff of five professionals.

Other Experience.
• BBH & Co., d.b.a. ENVIRONMENT AFFILIATED, **Executive Vice President**. Administered six-figure budget and supervised 27 managers. Directed recruitment and marketing activities.

• CSU Long Beach, **Development Director.** Managed $40 million dollar project to expand campus grounds 30%. Maintained lowest campus construction budget in state, including contracting and materials.

• TRADE ALTERNATIVE, **Commercial Properties Manager.** Marketed, leased, and acquired $900,000 in commercial property. Catered to such upscale clientele as high-end law firms.

Figure 10-1: This resume focuses on recent experience to avoid the problem of "overexperience."

The recent-experience-only spin doesn't work every time, but give it a try — it shows that you're not stuck in a time warp, and it's a better tactic than advertising your age as one that qualifies for carbon dating.

If the employer is notorious for hiring only young drafthorses, rethink your direction. Try to submit your resume to employers who can take advantage of your expertise, such as a new or expanding company operating in unfamiliar territory. Fortunately, a new tool has come along in the past several years admirably suited to this purpose: KickButt job hunters now turn to the Internet's discussion groups to check out job leads, to name names of saint and sinner companies, and to ask about company cultures and antidiscriminatory practices.

Based on your occupations, you can choose among the many thousands of discussion groups available through mailing lists (such as listserv's) and Usenet newsgroups. You may, for instance, want to connect with other architects, financial planners, or technical writers. To find them, use a search engine; you can start with c|net's search.com, (`http://www.search.com`), the "adoptive father of all search engines." This jumping-off place will lead to a number of main search engines, such as Infoseek, Lycos, and Alta Vista, and to specialized search engines found through the Web. The specialized engines include arts, automotive, business, computers, and so on.

In addition, the commercial online services — such as CompuServe, America Online, and Prodigy — offer a wide variety of forums and chat rooms that you can use to find out how others handled the perception problem you're facing.

If this method is unclear, read *Internet For Dummies*, published by IDG Books Worldwide.

What if the overqualified objection is just that and not a veil for age discrimination? The employer legitimately may be concerned that when something better comes along, you'll set a sprint record for shortest time on the job. Set your sights higher.

If you really prefer to take life easier or to have more time to yourself, you can be forthcoming with that fact in your resume's objective. Writing this kind of statement is tricky. You risk coming across as worn-out goods, ready to kick back and listen to babbling brooks while you collect a paycheck. When you explain your desire to back off an overly stressful work load, balance your words with a counterstatement reflecting your energy and commitment, as in this example:

Energetic and work-focused, but no longer enjoy frenzied managerial responsibility; seek a challenging nonmanagerial position.

Too much experience in one job

A reader writes:

> *I've stayed in my current and only job too long. When my company cut thou-sands of workers, we received outplacement classes. I was told that job overstayers are perceived to lack ambition, are not interested in learning new things, and are narrowly focused. What can I do about this?*

Spin strategy A: Divide your job into modules

Show that you successfully moved up and up, meeting new challenges and accepting ever more responsibility. Divide your job into realistic segments, which you label as Level 1, Level 2, Level 3, and so on. Describe each level as a separate position, just as you would if the levels had been different positions within the same company or with different employers. If your job titles changed as you moved up, that makes your writing task a lot easier.

Spin strategy B: Deal honestly with job titles

If your job title never changed, should you just make up job titles? No. The only truthful way to inaugurate fictional job titles is to parenthetically introduce them as "equivalent to …" Suppose that you are an accountant and have been in the same job for 25 years. Your segments might be titled like this:

- *Level 3 (equivalent to supervising accountant)*
- *Level 2 (equivalent to senior accountant)*
- *Level 1 (equivalent to accountant)*

To mitigate the lack of being knighted with increasingly senior job titles, fill your resume with references to your continuous salary increases and bonuses and the range of job skills you mastered.

Spin strategy C: Tackle deadly perceptions head on

Diminish any perception you became fat and sassy while staying in the same job too long by specifically describing open-ended workdays: "Worked past 5 p.m. at least once a week throughout employment." Derail the perception you don't want to learn new things by being specific in describing learning adven-tures: "Attended six semesters of word processing technologies; currently enrolled in adult education program to master latest software." Discount the perception you are narrowly focused by explaining that although your employ-ment address didn't change, professionally speaking, you are widely traveled in outside seminars, professional associations, and reading.

Spin strategy D: When nothing works, try something new

When you have followed the experts' recommendations note for note but are still sitting out the dance, take a chance on something new. In a departure from the normal practice of omitting from your resumes reasons for leaving a job, consider indicating why you're making a change after all this time. Neutralize the issue burning in every employer's mind: "Why now? Why after all these years are you on the market? Excessed out? Burned out?" If the question isn't asked, that doesn't mean it isn't hanging out in the recruiter's mind. Even though you may be seen as a moss-backed antiquity, reveal yourself as interested in today's and tomorrow's developments, by adding this kind of phrase in your objective:

- *Focusing on companies and organizations with contemporary viewpoints*

In an even more pioneering move to solve the same problem, create a whole new section at the tail of your resume, headed *Bright Future*, with a statement such as this:

BRIGHT FUTURE

Layoffs springing from a new management structure give me the welcomed opportunity to accept new challenges and freshen my worklife.

An employer's perception of highly experienced people may be that they are too rigid and hold expectations that the new environment will replicate the old — a perception that assassinates resumes. Not too long ago, a number of a blue-chip corporation's $75,000-a-year executive secretaries who had been there forever were axed; they had a problem with a capital *P*. Potential employers feared that not only could they not match former salaries, but also that the secretaries were spoiled by expecting high employee benefits and generous corporate practices.

If you're over 35 and sense that ageism or perceptions of rigidity are doing you in, defend yourself. Make your KickButt resume crackle with vitality, new words, and examples of your flexibility and motivation to learn. Create an image of your life as one of windows sliding open, not of doors creaking closed.

Too Little Experience

RezReaders root for conciseness because they want to cut to the chase. But new graduates often have the opposite problem — they need to beef up their entries — as this reader suggests:

My experience section looks emaciated. How can I feed it a little?

Writing your first resume is as much fun as cleaning out the garage. Assuming you're not a lazy person, one reason you don't get it done on time is fear — your value as a human being is reflected on a page, and that's scary. Either your life is too big to consolidate on paper or your life is nothing to brag about. Furthermore, you fear you can't write very well. Other than that, you've never done it before.

Deal with all these footdragging excuses by faithfully following the worksheet cues in Chapters 7 and 8. If you're not sure how your finished product should look, cast your eyes on Figure 10-2, which shows a hybrid formatted resume written by a new graduate who maximized a lean employment history.

New graduate with some experience

The word is trickling down that internships and student jobs are increasingly the ticket to the job market, as this question shows:

My school's career center is holding resume workshops for graduating seniors. I can't go because I'm doing as I was told — getting work experience. Do employers really believe that a student job produces valuable real-life experience?

Absolutely yes. A KickButt resume shows every shred of work experience, paid and unpaid, through internships, student jobs, co-op education, and extracurricular activities.

Stretching your experience is the spin, although you won't get away with claiming that you spent your summers as vice president of Microsoft.

Separate your jobs into fragments and explain them. For example, don't say that your job title was "office help" or "office clerk" and stop there. Divide the job into such functions as telephone reception, telephone sales, contract negotiations, purchasing, inventory, staff training, computer application training, public speaking, and written communications. Describe each one in terms of your accomplishments and their outcomes (see Chapter 7). Your inventory of worksheets like those you create in Chapter 7 is invaluable to pump up your experience without fibbing about it.

Figure 10-3 shows an example of before-and-after resumes that illustrates the spin on a moderate amount of work experience. A student wrote both versions and went on to be hired at a virtual magazine (online) in New York as an assistant art director.

> **NEW GRADUATE -- SOME EXPERIENCE**
>
> **MARTINA RABINOVICH**_____
>
> #543-B, College Drive, Boston, Massachusetts 45678, (910) 111-2131
>
> **OBJECTIVE**
> Position with environmentally and socially conscious public relations firm. Proven skills in public relations, research, and organization; demonstrated leadership qualities throughout university activities and professional experience. Computer Skills.
>
> **HIGHLIGHTS OF PUBLIC RELATIONS EXPERIENCE**
> _____
>
> - **House of Representatives Intern,** Renee H. Glamer's District Office, Elvin, MA. Summers 96-97
>   Assisted Representative Glamer to resolve constituents' issues. Communicated with legislative committees, researched legislation through the House computer system, and attended town meetings. Accumulated invaluable public relations skills using interpersonal abilities effectively in high-pressure, deadline-oriented situations. Major project: Veteran's Festival, 50th Anniversary.
>
> - **Student Body Vice-President,** Boston University, Boston, MA, 96-97
>   Chaired Council Operations Committee. Conducted all student body elections, using strong leadership and public speaking skills to accrue 1,600 votes.
>
> - **Medford Municipal Pool Lifeguard,** Medford, MA, Summers 90-96
>   Began as snack bar employee, earned certificate, promoted to lifeguard, and then to head lifeguard with managerial responsibilities. Supervised 11 employees.
>
> - **OTHER PUBLIC RELATIONS ACTIVITIES:**
>   Student advisor, tour guide, campus delegate, student ambassador for alumni, peer tutor for critical thinking.
>
> **RESEARCH EXPERIENCE**
> _____
>
> - **Republican Party Pollster,** Medford District, Medford, MA. May & Nov., 96 & 97
>   Distributed more than 50,000 sample ballots. Tabulated results, using math skills. Developed effective organizational skills, communicating with the general public and responding to their interests diplomatically.
>
> - **Medford County Historical Society Intern,** Medford County Historical Society, Medford, MA. Fall 96
>   Using practiced research skills, researched and designed an exhibit focusing on elections of Progressive party candidates. Exhibit is on display at Medford County Museum, visited by over 200 individuals a day.
>
> **ORGANIZATIONAL SKILLS**
> _____
>
> - **Alpha Kappa Omega Sorority Leader,** Boston University, Boston, MA, 95-97
>   Chaired Assault-Risk Management meetings, 96-97. Organized events to minimize individual and group risks of physical assault on campus. Assistant Bursar, 95-96. Used strong prioritizing and math skills to assist Treasurer in distribution of funds.

Figure 10-2: Sample resume of a new graduate.

> **NEW GRADUATE -- BEFORE**
>
> ### Dominic Preisendorfer
>
> 123 45th Way   Muhlenberg College
> Washington, OR. 67891   Box 321
> (011).121.3141   Allentown, PA 18104
>   (141)-312-1110
>
> **Education:**
> -Upper Washington High School: Graduated w/scholars diploma. Vice President of class.
>
> -Muhlenberg College, Allentown, PA
>   anticipate BA in spring 1998.
>   visual arts major with a concentration in graphic design involved w/campus arts festival.
>
> **Internships:**
> -Drury Design: Fall 1995 semester. Making mechanicals, layouts on computer, jersey design, research.
>
> -Washington Magazine (art dept.): Summer 1994. Assisted with layouts in the "well" of the front of the book.
>
> -Net Line Design: Spring 1993 semester. Helped in business side of office with filing, billing, typing. Prepared comps for presentation.
>
> **Work Experience:**
> -R.R. Manney: Fall 1990-current. Stock, sales, display, delivery
>
> Findings, summer 1990-95. Stock, sales, display
>
> **Computer Skills:**
>   Macintosh programs: Macwrite, Quark, PhotoShop, Aldus Freehand, Pagemaker,
>   Illustration IBM programs

Figure 10-3A: Even a thin-looking resume can be fleshed out.

Virtually no paid or unpaid experience

Need a job, get experience! Need experience, get a job! This predicament has frustrated new graduates since the polar ice caps retreated. Some graduates get the message almost too late. Frequently, a marginal new graduate not only drags along a low GPA (grade point average), say a 2.5, but has invested four or five years of non-school time developing skills as a television watcher, shopper, or socializer. The new graduate not only had no career-related internship or job but also didn't bother to get a job on restaurant row to fund such frivolities as kegs before finals and skiing afterward. There were no co-op assignments, no volunteer stints — zippo! This reader writes with a challenging query:

NEW GRADUATE -- AFTER

Dominic Preisendorfer

123 45th Way
Washington, Oregon 67891
(011) 121-3141

Muhlenberg College
Box 321
Allentown, PA 18104
(141) 312-1110

EDUCATION

Muhlenberg College, Allentown, Pennsylvania
BA, Art, June 1998. Chair, Campus Art Festival

INTERNSHIPS

Drury Design, Green Mills, Oregon
Fall 1995 semester
Contributed to all aspects of a cutting-edge, multi-faceted design firm.
- Researched trends as part of "Genie for the '90s" campaign. Drew sketches for new Genie: resulted as subject of article in New Yorker magazine.
- Developed mechanicals for U.S. Museum of Film Profiles magazine.
- Transformed BMX Bicycle Company's logo to evoke '90s image for racing jersey.
- Assisted with layout for the first Dark Horse style guide to be used by comics firms for licensing.

Washington Magazine, Washington, Oregon
Summer 1994
Assisted in day to day operations of the art department and in each aspect of production schedule.
- Helped evaluate and provide solutions for layouts in well of book.
- Contributed to redesign of book front. Recommended changes in type faces, colors, and sizes.

Net Line Design, Allentown, Pennsylvania
Spring 1993
Provided extensive clerical support for office, including billing, data entry, filing.
- Prepared samples for presentation.

WORK EXPERIENCE

Free-lance, Cafe Paradise, Green Mills, Oregon
Summer 1995
- Graphic Design: Designed logo, letterhead, business cards, and brochure.
- Advertising: Developed, implemented ad campaign including media purchasing.
- Interior Design: Worked with architect to design funky, eclectic bar, interior environment.

R.R. Manning, Washington, Oregon
Sales, Fall 1990-Present. High-end country furnishing and accessories store.
- Create windows and furniture displays, developing visual marketing skills and strategies.
- Servicing clients based on customer satisfaction and responses to marketing strategies.
- Train and supervise new hires in stocking and inventory.

COMPUTER SKILLS

- Macintosh Programs: Macwrite, Quark Express, Photoshop, Aldus Freehand, Pagemaker, Type Styler, Super Paint, and Illustrator.
- IBM Programs: Microsoft Publisher and Window Works.

Figure 10-3B: A new graduate adds a different spin.

I'm just a college brat — I have no experience, plus I didn't exactly distinguish myself with grades. How do I write a resume from air?

Having nothing but education to work with makes for a difficult resume scenario. Only dedicated job research and continual customizing of each resume has a chance of producing a KickButt product. Perhaps you've overlooked something; even child-sitting or pet-sitting offers experience in accepting responsibility and demonstrates reliability.

If an exhaustive search of your hobbies, campus activities, or community service turns up nothing worth putting on your resume, your education must carry the entire weight of candidacy for employment. Milk it dry, as the example in Figure 10-4 suggests.

Starting over with a master's degree

An advanced degree represents another kind of "too little experience" when you use it as a door-opener to a new career instead of continuing in your current field.

After career mishaps, many people see a master's degree as a born-again employment credential for a well-planned career change. And new beginnings often are the happy outcome. By contrast, if their goals were murky as baccalaureate graduates and are still murky as master's degree graduates, disappointed but better educated people fail to get what they want. The resume takes the brunt of the blame, as this question from a reader of my column suggests:

I am seeking a job with a new master's degree — obtained at age 47 — and experiencing a lot of difficulty. I have mailed out at least 500 resumes and received only one response — from a telephone company suggesting that I install telephone equipment. What is wrong with my resume?

The resume isn't the real problem here. If he sent the same resume to 500 potential employers, he's clearly not focused on what he's best fit to do — one size does not fit all. This individual should learn a great deal more about job hunting and then write a career plan to be reviewed monthly. *Job Hunting For Dummies* from IDG Books Worldwide, Inc., is a good place to start.

Returning to the resume treatment, if your master's degree is intended to facilitate a career change, see the career-transition resume discussion in Chapter 12. If your master's degree upgrades your credentials in the same field in which you now work, begin your resume by reporting your work experience; follow up with the education section, leading off with the newly minted master's degree. Make use of a resume-ending section titled *Other Information* to say that you view learning as a life-skill, as evidenced by the master's degree.

NEW GRADUATE -- LITTLE EXPERIENCE

Deanna R. McNealy
(111) 213-1415

1234 University Drive, # 56 B
Irvine, California 78910

Seek entry-level retail sales position. Offer more than three years' intensive study of public communication. Completed Bachelor's degree, developing strong research, language, interpersonal, computer and disciplinary skills. Proven interactive skills with groups and individuals. Energetic, adaptive, fast learner.

BACKGROUND & EDUCATION

• **Bachelor of Arts, University of California at Irvine (UCI), May, 1997, Literature & Social Studies**

Self-Directed Studies   1995-Present
Focusing on mainstream culture and trends, study merchandising and population demographics of individuals between the ages of 18 and 49. Browse media and advertising extensively, developing an in-depth understanding of material consumption in U.S. culture.

University Studies
8/1- 12/29, 1996   Literary Philosophy, Graduate, UCI, Irvine, California
Accumulated skills in prioritizing, self-management and discipline, accomplishing over 90 pages of commentary on the subject of philosophical thought.

1/23 - 5/25, 1996   Social Text and Context, UCI, Irvine, California
Developed in-depth understanding of public consensus and modern value systems. Concentration: the relationship between ideals and historical and economic patterns.

1/23 - 5/25, 1996   Critical Thinking, UCI, Irvine, California
60 hours of self-directed research and lecture attendance, studying essential elements of critical thought. Developed skills in argumentative dialogue, logic, analysis, and approaching perception from an educated and diverse perspective. Focus: anatomy of critical thought.

1/23, 1995 - 5/25, 1996   Public Communication, UCI, Irvine, California
Intensive study of the psychological and social techniques of speech and communication. Developed comprehensive understanding of debate, physical language, formal and informal delivery, subliminal communication, and advertising. Focus: written and visual advertising techniques.

Other Experience   1995 - Present, UCI, Irvine, California
15th and 16th Century Rhetoric, French Poetry, Literature in Music, Women, Words & Wisdom, Film Theory, Shakespeare, British Fiction, U.S. Fiction, World Literature.

SKILLS
Computer: All word processing applications on Macintosh and IBM, Internet savvy.
Interpersonal: Experienced in working with groups and individuals, using teamwork and collaboration, setting goals, delegating and communicating effectively.

Figure 10-4: The resume of a graduate with little experience.

When the Ph.D. is a liability

You slaved and skimped in school to earn a doctorate. Now that you're seeking to use that knowledge and credential, your head is being thrust into a brick wall. This dilemma calls for all the critical thinking faculties you developed in your educational pursuits, as this plaintive appeal reveals:

But … I went through six years of learning at tough schools, and now that I'm $80,000 in debt for my Ph.D., nobody wants to hire me. Isn't my education supposed to insure my employment?

Unfortunately, that's not how it works. A doctorate traditionally has been reserved for research or teaching, but even those job prospects aren't living up to expectations. Doctorate-holding job hunters return day after day with reports of rejection because they are said to be "overqualified." Here are two viewpoints on this issue:

✔ From a career adviser to Ph.D.s: "Although the job market for Ph.D.s is tight, disastrously so in some fields, unemployment rates are very low, and those earning doctorates almost always end up in professional positions that use their intelligence, if not their training. It may take a few years to find their niches."

✔ From an outplacement consultant: "Ph.D.s are hard to place. Companies assume they will not be contented in a job that doesn't make use of their education. If they are older, it is twice as hard. Many companies have given up their R&D (research and development) labs.

"Universities look for someone who can bring in grant money. I ask Ph.D.s to make two resumes — one with the degree and one without. The one without at least gets them interviews."

View number two gets my vote because not everyone has several years to launch a career. Although it's disheartening, I suggest that, unless you are certain a Ph.D. is required for the position(s), you omit the Piled High and Deep degree from your resume.

As I discuss in Chapter 5, you are not writing an autobiography but rather a selected view of your strengths as they apply to the job market.

Too Long Gone: For Women Only

The reentering woman still has it tough. Usually, it's Mom who puts her career on hold to meet family responsibilities. When she tries to reenter the job market, by choice or economic necessity, she feels as though she's been living on another planet, as this letter shows:

Employers don't want to hire women if they've been mothers and out of the market for more than a year or two. Hey, ya'know, for the last 10 years, I've worked my tail off! Don't they understand that? Doesn't intelligence, willingness to work hard, creativity, attention to detail, drive, efficiency, grace under pressure, initiative, leadership, persistence, resourcefulness, responsibility, teamwork, and a sense of humor mean anything these days?

Every characteristic that this reader mentions is still a hot ticket in the job market, but the burden is on her to interpret these virtues as marketable skills.

- ✔ Grace under pressure, for example, translates to *crisis manager,* a valuable person when the electricity fails in a computer-driven office.
- ✔ Resourcefulness translates to *office manager,* who is able to ward off crank calls from credit collection agencies.
- ✔ A sense of humor translates to *data communications manager,* who joshes a sleepy technical whiz into reporting for work at two in the morning for emergency repair of a busted satellite hovering over Europe.

Here's what the returning woman must do to develop a KickButt resume that connects what she can do with what an employer wants done.

Look back in discovery

Review your worksheets to spot transferable skills that you gained in volunteer, civic, hobby, and domestic work. Scout for adult and continuing education, both on campus and in nontraditional settings.

Reexamine the informative television programs you've watched, the news magazines you've monitored. Go the library and read business magazines and trade journals to make a lexicon of up-to-date words, such as *Please compare my skills* (not *I'm sure you will agree*).

Avoid tired words like *go-getter* and *upwardly mobile.* Yesteryear's buzzwords, such as *management by objective* and *girl Friday* won't do a thing to perk up your image.

Incorporate professional terms

The use of professional words can help de-emphasize informal training or work experience. But you must be careful when doing this to show good judgment about the work world.

Professionalizing your domestic experience is a tightrope walk: Ignoring it leaves you looking like a missing person, yet you can't be pretentious or naive. Don't say *housewife;* say *family caretaker* or *domestic specialist.* Refer to *home management* to minimize gaps in time spent as a homemaker. **Important:** Fill the home management period with transferable skills relevant to the targeted position.

Delve into what you did during your home management period. You did not hold a paid job, but you did do important unpaid work. Dissect your achievements to find your deeds — they can be impressive. Examples range from time management (developing the ability to do more with less time) to budgeting experience (developing a sophisticated understanding of priority allocation of financial resources). Other examples include using the telephone in drumming up support for a favorite charity (developing confidence and a businesslike telephone technique) and leadership positions in the PTA (developing a sense of authority and the ability to guide others).

Despite two decades of media attention to skills developed by homemakers, employers continue to be dismissive of parenting and other abilities acquired inside the home. Many employers believe identifying yourself as a domestic specialist is no more workplace-useful than claiming to be a "seasoned husband" or "experienced friend."

Make your homemaker skills difficult to disrespect by showing their relevance to a given career field. Be careful to avoid sounding as though you attended a workshop where you memorized big words.

Whatever you do, you can't ignore the issue — like where have you been for the past few years? When you lack skills developed outside the home in community work, you have to do the best you can to pull out home-based skills.

Selected home-based skills

Don't overlook these skills you may have acquired inside the home. I've included a few examples of occupations in which they can be used. This illustration assumes you lack formal credentials for professional-level work. If you do have the credentials, upgrade the examples to the appropriate job level.

✔ **Juggling schedules:** Paraprofessional assistant to business executives, physicians. Small-service business operator, dispatching staff of technicians.

✔ **Peer counseling:** Human resources department employee benefits assistant. Substance abuse program manager.

✔ **Arranging social events:** Party shop manager. Nonprofit organization fund-raiser. Art gallery employee.

✔ **Conflict resolution:** Administrative assistant. Customer service representative. School secretary.

✔ **Problem-solving.** Any job.

✔ **Decorating:** Interior decorator. Interior fabric shop sales person.

✔ **Nursing:** Medical or dental office assistant.

✔ **Solid purchasing judgment:** Purchasing agent. Merchandiser.

✔ **Planning trips, relocations:** Travel agent. Corporate employee relocation coordinator.

✔ **Communicating:** Any job.

✔ **Shaping budgets:** Office manager. Department head. Accounting clerk.

✔ **Maximizing interior spaces:** Commercial-office real estate agent. Business furniture store operator.

Use years or use dates — not both

Some advisers suggest that in referring to your home management years, you use years, not dates, which avoids the gap in paid work experience, like so:

- *Family Care, 10 years*

  Child care, home operations, budgeting and support for a family of four. Participation in parent/school relations, human services, and religious organization

- *Leadership Positions*

  Vice President, Curriculum Committee, PTA; Chair, Fund-Raising, American Humane Society; Subcommittee Chair, Budget Committee, First Baptist Church.

This *years-only approach* is unlikely to make a favorable impression on a person who hires often. Employment professionals prefer concrete facts and dates. But the years-only resume can work at small businesses where the hiring manager also wears several other hats and doesn't pay much attention to hiring guidelines.

Don't make the mistake of using both forms on the same resume, assigning dates to your paid jobs but only years to your homemaker work.

Showcase your best work: an example

Figure 10-5 shows a resume sample of interest to re-entering women.

Know the score

Gender bias lives, and, of course, you should omit all information that the employer is not entitled to, including your age, marital status, physical condition, number and ages of children, and husband's name. Even though the law is on your side, in today's interview-rationed job market, your resume must qualify you more than the next guy. If you've been out of the job market for some years, you have to work harder and smarter to show you're a hot hire. You may want to seek out seminars and services offered to re-entering women to help in your quest.

RE-ENTRY

JOY R. NGUYEN

12 Watt Road, Palmira, Florida 34567   (321) 654-9876

SUMMARY OF EXPERIENCE
More than five years' experience in event-planning, fundraising, administration and publicity. More than nine years' experience in administration for retail and manufacturing firms. B.A. in Business. Florida Teaching Certificate.

NONPROFIT/VOLUNTEER SERVICE

1995-Present   Palmira Optimists' Association, Palmira, Florida
Membership Committee Chair
Planning, organizing programs, exhibits and events to recruit association members. Coordinated annual new member events.

1987-1997   Okeefenokee County Y.M.C.A., Okeefenokee, Florida
Member, Board of Directors and Executive Committee
Spearheaded first Y.M.C.A. organization in county. Designed programs, procedures, and policies, monitoring trustees in the construction of $3 million facility. Led $2.5 million fundraising campaign.

• **Fundraising Chair**, 1990-1996 Raised funds for entire construction project, establishing hundreds of donors and supervising project. Sourced contractors and directed fundraising activities, using strong interpersonal and networking skills.

HOME MANAGEMENT EXPERIENCE

• **Scheduling**: Assisted business executive and two children in the scheduling of travel and 160,000 miles of transportation. Arranged ticketing, negotiated finances of $12,000 in travel expenses.
• **Conflict Resolution**. Arbitrated personal, business issues. Effective interpersonal skills.
• **Relocation**: Launched inter-state relocation of entire family, coordinating moving services, trucks, and packing schedules.
• **Budget & Purchasing**: Managed family finances, including budgeting, medical, dental, insurance packages, two home purchases, three auto purchases, expenses and taxes. Developed finance and math skills.

ADDITIONAL PROFESSIONAL EXPERIENCE
1987-1989   Sunrise Books, Cabana, Florida
Assistant Manager, Sales Representative
Managed daily operations of coffee house and bookstore, directing staff of 35. Supervised entire floor of merchandise and stock. Purchased all side-line goods.

• Spearheaded store's first sales campaign, resulting in tripled sales.
• Designed system for inventory analysis, streamlining purchasing and display control.
• Redirected staff duties for more effective work hours.
• Promoted from sales to supervisor in 38 days; three months later to asst. mgr.

EDUCATION
• **Bachelor of Science in Business**, 1987, University of Miami, Miami, G.P.A.: 3.75
• **Florida Teaching Certificate**, Business and English, 1994, Florida State, Palmira

Figure 10-5: Sample resume of a domestic specialist re-entering the work world.

Spin Control Is in the Details

A white ruffled blouse stained only slightly with one dab of spaghetti sauce is 99 percent clean. But every person who sees me wear it remembers the red spot, not the rest of the blouse. You can have a 99 percent KickButt resume, but any one of the deadly perceptions identified in this chapter can ice it without your knowing why. Practice spin control — present possible negative perceptions in a flattering light.

Chapter 11
Spin Control of Special Issues

* *

In This Chapter

▶ Guarding against negative information

▶ Dealing with disability issues

▶ Patching over employment gaps

▶ Spin-controlling a demotion

▶ Adding focus to the overpopulated resume

▶ Constructing resume-accessory references

* *

Chapter 10 focuses on KickButt spin-control techniques that apply to various aspects of experience, a traditional issue that affects most people during their lifetime. In this chapter, I examine selected special issues that concern fewer people but can be most difficult to handle. Spin control will help you over the hump of a variety of problems that, until now, you rarely had to confront.

Some issues, such as disability or criminal justice problems, may never relate to you. Other issues, such as job tenure, have gained new urgency in an era when more and more companies buy your brains and skills for a period of time and then cut you loose.

I know a few people with a "perfect" job history — but only a few. Most job seekers are burdened with special issues that won't survive a standard-issue resume. Here are spin-control techniques for various resume predicaments and concerns.

Omit Inappropriate Data Points

The best way to handle some land mines on your resume is to ignore them.

As explained in Chapter 5, conventional wisdom advises that it's a mistake to reveal negative information on a resume. Save trouble-making information for the all-important job interview, where you have a fighting chance to explain your side of things.

Generally speaking, stay away from these topics when constructing a resume:

- ✔ Firings, demotions, forced resignations, and early termination of contracts
- ✔ Personal differences with coworkers or supervisors
- ✔ Bankruptcy, tax evasion, or credit problems
- ✔ Criminal convictions or lawsuits
- ✔ Homelessness
- ✔ Illnesses from which you have now recovered
- ✔ Disabilities that do not prevent you from performing the essential functions of the job, with or without some form of accommodation

Should you ever give reasons for leaving a job?

In most instances, resume silence in the face of interview-killing facts is still the strategy of choice. But the time has come to rethink at least one special issue: losing a job.

Now that jobs are being shed like so many autumn leaves, losing a job is no longer viewed as a case of personal failure. It may be to your advantage to state on your resume why you left your last position, assuming that it was not due to poor work performance on your part. If you were downsized out, the RezReader may appreciate your straightforward statement "Job eliminated in downsizing."

But remember, if you elect to say why you lost one job, for consistency you have to say why you left all your jobs — such as for greater opportunity, advancement, and the like.

Job Seekers with Disabilities

More than 40 million Americans are protected by the ADA (Americans with Disabilities Act), which covers a wide spectrum of disabilities. These disabilities include acquired immunodeficiency syndrome (AIDS) and human immunodeficiency virus (HIV), alcoholism, cancer, cerebral palsy, diabetes, emotional illness, epilepsy, hearing and speech disorders, heart disorders, learning disabilities such as dyslexia, mental retardation, muscular dystrophy, and visual impairments. The act does not cover conditions that impose short-term limitations, such as pregnancy or broken bones.

The ADA makes it illegal for an employer to refuse to hire (or discriminate against) a person simply because that person has one or more disabilities. Generally, the ADA forbids employers who have more than 15 employees and who are hiring from doing the following:

- ✔ Discriminate on the basis of any physical or mental disability
- ✔ Ask job applicants questions about their past or current medical conditions
- ✔ Require applicants to take pre-employment medical exams

The ADA requires that an employer make reasonable accommodations for qualified individuals who have disabilities, unless doing so would cause the employer "undue hardship." The undue hardship provision is still open to interpretation by the courts.

If you have a disability that you believe is covered by the ADA, familiarize yourself with the law's specifics. Call your member of Congress, visit your library, or obtain free comprehensive ADA guides and supporting materials from the splendid Internet World Wide Web site maintained by the Job Accommodation Network (http://janweb.icdi.wvu.edu/).

The ADA watches your back to prevent discrimination based on your disability, but RezReaders may still weasel around the law to avoid what they perceive as a liability. Use street savvy: When you can't win and you can't break even, change the game.

In your game, spin control begins with not disclosing your disability on your resume.

When should you disclose your disability?

- ✔ If your disability is visible, the best time to disclose it is after the interview has been set and you telephone to confirm the arrangements. Pass the message in an offhanded manner: "Because I use a wheelchair for mobility, I was wondering if you can suggest which entrance to your building would be the most convenient?"
- ✔ Alternatively, you may want to reserve disclosure for the interview.
- ✔ If your disability is not visible, such as mental illness or epilepsy, you need not disclose it unless you'll need special accommodations. Even then, you can hold the disclosure until the negotiating stage once you've received a potential job offer.

Either way, be confident, unapologetic, unimpaired, and attitude-positive. Disclosure in the job-search process is a complex quandary; for a comprehensive discussion, I recommend Melanie Astaire Witt's book *Job Strategies for People With Disabilities* (Peterson's).

What can you do about gaps in your work history caused by disability?

In years past, you might have been able to obscure the issue. No longer. New computer databases make it easy for suspicious employers to research your medical history. And with health insurance costs so high, they may do exactly that. If your illness-related job history has so many gaps that it looks like a hockey player's teeth, I've never heard a better suggestion than writing the no-pretense "Illness and Recovery" next to the date. It's honest, and the "recovery" part says, "I'm back and ready to work!"

If you have too many episodes of "missing teeth," your work history will look less shaky in a functional format, discussed in Chapter 2. Online resume discussion groups, which you can find through the Job Accommodation Network, are further sources of guidance on this difficult issue.

Finally, should you mention on your resume a need for adaptive equipment, such as a special kind of telephone?

I wouldn't mention the need for adaptive equipment — even if the equipment is inexpensive or you're willing to buy it yourself. Instead, stick with the time-release-capsule method of sharing information: Dribble out those revelations that may stifle interest in hiring you only when necessary. Never lose sight of your objective: to get an interview.

When Demotion Strikes

Kevin Allen (real person, phony name) was the district manager of five stores in a chain when he was demoted to manager of a single store. The chain was sending him a message — the chain's top managers hoped he'd quit so they could avoid awarding a severance package of benefits. Kevin ignored the message, retained a lawyer, kept his job, and started a job hunt after hours.

He finessed his resume by listing all the positions he had held in the chain, leaving out dates of when each started and stopped. Achievements were combined.

Demoting Store Chain, Big City

> *District Manager, 5 stores*
>
> *Store Manager, Windy City*
>
> *Store Assistant Manager, Sunny City*
>
> *Store Clerk, Sunny City*

Throwing all of Kevin's titles into one big pot seemed a clever idea, but it didn't work for him. After a year of searching, Kevin got interviews, yes; but at every single face-to-face meeting, he was nailed with the same question: "Why were you demoted?" The interviewers' attitudes seemed accusatory, as if they'd been misled. Kevin failed to answer the question satisfactorily — he did not receive a single offer during a year's search. How did all the potential employers find out the truth?

Among obvious explanations: (A) Kevin worked in a "village" industry where people know each other and gossip. (B) Employers ordered credit checks on him; credit checks show employment details. (C) Employers authorized private investigations, an uncommon but not unheard-of practice in private business.

No one knows what really happened, but in hindsight, Kevin might have done better had he accepted the message that the chain wanted him out, negotiated a favorable severance package that included good references, and quit immediately while his true title was that of district manager.

After two humiliating years of demotion status, Kevin took action by "crossing the River Jordan," a Biblical phrase that universities have adapted. It refers to those who seek a new beginning by returning to college for a law or business degree. Kevin enrolled in law school.

In cases like Kevin's, a strategy that may work better is forthright but doesn't flash your demotion in neon lights. Combine only two titles together, followed quickly by your accomplishments and strengths:

1994 - 1997 Demoting Company Name

> Assistant Manager, Manager

As assistant manager, supported the manager and carefully monitored detailed transactions with vendors, insuring maintenance of products and inventory; used skills in invoicing, billing, ordering, and purchasing. As manager, supervised all aspects of purchasing, display, and merchandise sales. Trained team of more than 30 employees in two-week period. Trained three assistant managers in essential functions of customers, employees, and finance. Increased sales revenues 25 percent in first six months.

No matter how well you handle your resume entry, the reference of the demoting employer may ultimately end your chances of landing a new job that you want. In trying to mend fences, you may appeal to the demoting employer's fairness or go for guilt. Point out how hard you worked and how loyal you've been. Find reasons why your performance record was flawed. Ask for the commitment of a favorable reference and a downplaying of the demotion. If fairness or guilt appeals are denied, see an employment lawyer about sending the demoting employer, on law-firm letterhead, a warning against libel or slander.

The basic way to handle demotions throughout the job-hunting process is akin to how you handle being fired: by accentuating the positive contributions and results for which you are responsible. *But being demoted is trickier to handle than being fired.* It's a weirdish fact, but being fired no longer suggests personal failure; being demoted does.

Sealing Gaps in Your Record

Periods of unemployment leave black holes in your work history. Should you (A) fill them with positive expressions such as *family obligations,* (B) fill them with less positive but true words such as *unemployed,* or (C) show the gap without comment?

Choosing B, *unemployed,* is dreary. Forget that! Choosing C, *leave-it-blank-and-say-nothing,* often works — just hope it won't be noticed. My choice is A: Tell the truth about what you were doing but spin-control it in a dignified, positive way. A few examples: *independent study ... foreign travel ... career renewal through study and assessment.*

An infoblizzard of tips has been published on how to repair resume holes. Unless you were building bombs in a terrorist training camp, the principles are simple:

- ✔ Present the time gap as a positive event.

- ✔ Detail why it made you a better worker — not a better *person,* but a better worker with more favorable characteristics, polished skills, and mature understanding, all of which you're dying to contribute to your new employer.

How can these principles be applied? Take the case of a student who dropped out of college to play in a band and do odd jobs for four years before coming back to finish his biology degree and look for a job. The student knows that employers may perceive him as not committed to a career. In the resume, he should treat the band years like any other job: Describe the skills that were polished as a band leader. Identify instances of problem solving, teamwork, leadership, and budgeting.

The real problem solver has to come in the cover letter that accompanies this resume, as Abilene Christian University Director of Career Services Jack Stewart outlines:

> *After completing two years of undergraduate study, it was necessary for me to work to continue my education. Using my talents as a musician, I organized a band and after four years was able to continue my education. I matured and learned much about the real world and confirmed that an education is extremely important in fulfilling my career goals.*

The chief mistake people make is assuming that a positive explanation won't sell and fudging dates from legitimate jobs to cover the black holes. You may get away with it in the beginning. But ultimately, you will be asked to sign a formal application, a legal document. When a company wishes to chop staff without paying severance benefits, the first thing that happens is an intense investigation of the company's database of application forms. People who lied on their applications can be sent out into the mean streets with nothing but their current paychecks on their backs.

Lying just isn't worth the risk.

The consultant/entrepreneur gap

Professional and managerial job seekers are routinely advised to explain black holes by saying that they were consultants or that they owned small businesses. Not everyone can be a consultant, and there's substantial risk in the small-business explanation.

If it should happen to be true that you were a consultant, name your clients and give a glimmer of the contributions you made to each. If you really had a small business, remember: Employers worry that you'll be too independent to do things their way, or that you'll stay just long enough to learn their business and go into competition against them. **Strategic antidotes:** Search for a business owner who is within eyeshot of retirement and wouldn't mind your continuing the business and paying a monthly pension. **Resume antidotes:** Describe yourself as "manager," not "CEO" or "president," and if you have time, rename your business something other than your own name: "River's End Associates, Inc.," not "Theresa K. Bronz, Inc."

Another method of papering-over glaring gaps is to include all your work under "Work History" and cite unpaid and volunteer work as well as paid jobs.

Suppose you've been unemployed for the past year. That's a new black hole. Some advisers suggest the old dodge of allowing the RezReader to misperceive the open-ended date of employment for your last job: "1995 - " as though you meant "1995 - Present." The open-ender solution often works — until you run into a RezReader who thinks it's way too calculating.

Black holes are less obvious in a functional format, as discussed in Chapter 2. *If you can't find a positive explanation for a black hole, say nothing.*

Application forms: take them seriously

Although many job hunters tend to blow off formal application forms, these tiresome profiles are legal documents. Lies can come back to bite you. Stick to the facts as you follow these rules and push some paper:

- If allowed, take the application home; photocopy it in case you spill coffee on your first effort.

- Verify all dates of employment and salaries to the letter.

- Enter the full name and last known address of former employers. If former employers are no longer available, don't substitute coworkers.

- If asked for salary history, give your base salary (or plus commission), omitting benefits.

- Give a complete employment history in months and years, including trivial three-week jobs that you wisely left off the resume. If you stint on telling the whole story, you leave a loophole of withholding information that later can be used against you if the employer decides you're excess.

- Unless you have a condition directly affecting your ability to do the job for which you are applying, you need not elaborate on it.

- Divulge any criminal record unless your records are sealed; consult a lawyer before job hunting.

- Be honest about having collected unemployment benefits (but remember that purposeful repeaters are frowned on); if you're caught lying about it later, practice your farewell speech.

- Autograph the application; you have been honest — why worry?

If you possess a not-so-pristine past, stick with small employers who probably won't dig into the minutiae.

Here a Job, There a Job, Everywhere a Job, Job

I once interviewed a man who had held 185 jobs over the course of his 20-year career, ranging from dishwasher to circus clown, and from truck driver to nursing aid.

He wrote to me, not requesting resume advice, but to complain that a potential employer had the nerve to call him a *job hopper*!

Talk about an antiquated term — in the late 20th century, the notion of job hopping is as far out of a reality circle as the concepts of job security, company loyalty, and a guaranteed company pension. The Great American Dumping Machine will continue to sack people who then will take virtually any job they can to survive.

The risk of having too many jobs in your background is one of focus. *Unfocused* is an ugly word in job-search circles. Being judged as "unfocused" is saying that you lack commitment, that you are perpetually at a fork in the road. It's a reason not to hire you.

The jobs-impacted resume problem is exploding, affecting large numbers of people. A twentysomething intern in my office says everyone she knows has already had "too many jobs." The harsh realities of business are forcing people to detour from a single career pathway to the acquisition of new skills and experiences, even if they are not skills and experiences of choice. Serious creative writing will be needed to keep a resume focus on the work history that is relevant for the next job sought.

Many superbly talented and hard-working job hunters today have too many jobs in their history by circumstance, not by choice. If you're in this cohort,

- ✔ Start by referring to your *diversified* background.
- ✔ Use a functional or hybrid resume format, presenting *only your experience relevant to the job you seek.*
- ✔ Express your work history in years, not months and years.

When your resume looks as though it will collapse under the weight of a mishmash of jobs unconnected to your present target, eliminate your previous trivial pursuits. Group the consequential jobs under a heading that says, *Relevant Work Experience Summary.*

What if this approach solves one problem — the overpopulated resume — but creates another, such as a huge, gaping black hole where you removed inconsequential jobs? Create a second work history section that covers those holes, labeling it "Other Experience." Figure 11-1 shows an example.

IMPACTED RESUME WITH FOCUS

Professional Experience

UNITECH, Hamburg, Germany
Computer Laboratory Assistant, 1995-Present
> Manage and troubleshoot hardware and software systems. Recover data, create programming
> architecture, and install parts and software. Assist a team of 18 engineers.

TECHNIK TECH, Hamburg, Germany
Assistant to System Analysts, 1991 - 1994
> Participated in construction, repair, and installation of systems at local businesses. Diagnosed faulty systems and reported to senior analysts, decreasing their work load by 25%.

TRADE NET, Berlin, Germany
Applications and Network Specialist, 1989-1991
> Set up and monitored a Windows based BBS, including installation, structure, security, and graphics. Authored installation scripts for Trade Net, licensing U.S. software use in Europe.

Other Experience

AMERICAN TOY STORE, Berlin, Germany, Sales Representative, 1994-1995
Arranged and inventoried merchandise, directed sales and customer relations. Developed strong interpersonal skills and gained knowledge of retail industry.

CAMP INTERNATIONAL, Oslo, Germany, Activities Director, 1989-1991
Organized daily activities for more than 300 children from English-speaking countries, including sports, recreation, and day classes. Supervised 10 counselors and kitchen staff of five, developing responsible and effective management skills.

Figure 11-1: Solving the black-hole problem in a jobs-impacted resume by creating a focus plus a second work history section.

Dealing with an unfocused career pattern on paper is easier when it's done under the banner of a temporary service company. The spin in this case lists the temporary services company as the employer. You choose one job title that covers most of your assignments. Under that umbrella title, identify specific assignments. Give the dates in years next to the temporary services firm, skipping dates for each assignment. Figure 11-2 shows an example.

What if you work for several temporary services at the same time? The simple answer is that you use the same technique of dating your work history for the temporary service firms, not for the individual assignments. This dating technique is a statement of fact; you legally are an employee of the temporary services firm, not of the company that pays for your temporary services.

FOCUSING WITH TEMP JOBS

Professional Experience

Relia-Temps   1995-present

Executive Secretary

- North Western Banking Group,
Perform all clerical and administrative responsibilities for 10-partner investment
and loan firm, assisting each partner in drafting contracts, reviewing proposals, and
designing various financial programs. Supervise 7 staff members. Introduced 50%
more efficient filing system, reducing client reviews from 4 to 3 hours.

Administrative Assistant

- Mosaic Advertising,
Supervised 3 receptionists and 4 clerical specialists, reporting directly to president.
Administered daily operations of all accounting and communication transactions.
Using extensive computer savvy, upgraded company computer networks with
Windows '95.

- Blakeslee Environmental, Inc.,
Assisted 8 attorneys at interstate environmental protection agency, scheduling
meetings and conferences, maintaining files, and updating database records.
Redesigned office procedures and methods of communication, employing

Figure 11-2:
Listing your
temporary
job
assignments
without
looking
unfocused.

When Substance Abuse Is the Problem

Substance abuse is a disability under the Americans with Disabilities Act. If you
are recovered from the addiction, you are entitled to all of the Act's protections.
If you are still abusing a substance, such as alcohol or illegal narcotics, you are
not covered by the Act. Do not disclose previous substance abuse on your
resume.

Cover gaps in your work history with the "Illness and Recovery" statement (see
the "Job Seekers with Disabilities" section of this chapter) or simply do not
address the issue at all. Be careful what you put on a job application form —
remember that it is a legal form and that lies can come back to haunt you (see
the "Sealing Gaps in Your Record" section of this chapter).

If you were ever arrested for smoking pot or being intoxicated — even once in
your life — the fact may surface to damage your employment chances. Asking
about arrest records is illegal, but a few private companies don't let that stop
them — they compile electronic databases of such arrest information and sell
them to employers.

The upshot: Avoid a resume mention of booze or drugs, be careful about
application forms, and be honest at interviews — *if* you have recovered or *if* the
experience was a brief fling or two. If you are still held prisoner by a chronic,

destructive, or debilitating overuse of a chemical substance that interferes with your life or employment, no resume tweaks will benefit you. Get help for your addiction.

Suggestions for Inmates and Ex-Inmates

The best resume advice for prison inmates is to get additional education, not only for education's sake but because you can explain gaps with it. You could, for example, write "1990 - 95 Bachelor's in Education, Regents College, New York." (Regents is a highly regarded distance learning university.)

If you're an ex-inmate and you missed out on educational opportunities, write what you did during your incarceration — cook, carpenter, clerk, and so forth. Listing "1985 - 1997 Masonry Foreman" beats "1985 - 1997 Alcatraz Penitentiary."

The strategy to use on your resume is to show that you made constructive use of your time during your lockup.

Ask your prison administrator or parole officer to refer you to nonprofit organizations that provide employment assistance to former offenders. A comprehensive work on the subject is *The Ex-Inmate's Complete Guide to Successful Employment* by Errol Craig Sull, available by mail from The Correctional Education Company, 370 Franklin St., Buffalo, NY 14202; phone 716-849-0247.

References Gain New Importance

Do not include your references on your resume. Do create a second document filled with the names and correct telephone numbers and addresses of references. Supply this sheet only when requested by an interested potential employer — don't burn out your references by allowing too many casual callers access to their names and contact information.

With job changes on the upswing throughout the developed world, the matter of references is hooked up to your KickButt job search like it's your kidney dialysis machine. In an earlier time, when supply and demand were roughly in balance, employers didn't always bother to check references. Small employers still may not, but mid-sized and large companies, afraid of making a hiring mistake, are taking aim on your past. Reference-auditing companies that specialize in uncovering reasons not to hire candidates contract with employers.

Rules vary slightly in different states, but employers can legally investigate not only references but an applicant's credit history, record of criminal convictions (not arrests), moving violations and accidents, performance at previous jobs, and workers' compensation claims.

Because so much information is available about you — probably more than you or I think about, according to recent privacy invasion books — make a project of handling your references. Key suggestions include the following:

- ✔ **Choose your references carefully.** List references who have direct knowledge of your job performance. If necessary, go beyond your immediate supervisor and include past or present coworkers, subordinates, customers, suppliers, members of trade associations, or anyone else who can praise your work. With the exception of your immediate boss, never — *never* — list a reference until you have gained that person's permission to do so. Make a dry run: Have a brave buddy call your references to make certain that no sly naysayers are hiding behind friendly faces.

- ✔ **Coach your references.** Providing your resume is standard operating procedure. Go further: Write a short script of likely questions with a summary of persuasion points under each question. In addition to general good words about your industriousness, creativity, and leadership, focus on the industry. If you're applying at a financial institution, suggest that your references dwell on trustworthiness, conservatism, and good judgment. If you're applying at a high tech company that has proprietary software and inventions, ask your references to stress your ethics and loyalty.

- ✔ **Write your own reference letters.** A letter of reference is not particularly effective, but it is better than nothing in cases where a company tanks out, your boss dies, or the reference is difficult to reach. When you want a reference letter, go after it KickButt style: Offer to draft or even to prepare for signature a letter of praise on your reference's letterhead. Routinely arrange for a reference letter when you leave a job.

- ✔ **Stamp out bad references.** If you were axed or pressed to resign, or you told your boss what you thought and flat-out quit, move immediately from spin control to damage control. Even if you were cool enough to obtain a letter of reference before you left, you absolutely must gulp down the bile and try at minimum to neutralize the reference.

As mentioned earlier in this chapter, appeal to a sense of fair play or guilt. Sometimes just saying you are sorry and you hope the employer won't keep you from earning a living will be enough. Sometimes it won't.

When you have done all you can to overcome a bad reference, you have three options:

✔ Drown the poor reference in large numbers of favorable references.

✔ Find a lawyer who, for $100 or so, will write a letter threatening legal action for libel or slander. This approach is surprisingly effective.

✔ Continue your job hunt, concentrating on small firms that may not check references or who may be more inclined to take a chance on someone.

No matter how super-powerful you've made your resume, weak or poor references can wipe out your job chances. That's why you write the sample question-and-answer scripts and the reference letters, and that's why you take the first step to patch things up with former adversaries. Your employment is a much higher priority by far to you than it is to reference-givers.

Positive Statements Draw Interest

A positive explanation goes a long way in overcoming a resume land mine. It won't work all the time, but it will work some of the time, and all you need — for now — is one good offer to hit the job jackpot.

Chapter 12

Core Concepts for Career Changers Today

· ·

In This Chapter

▶ New motivations for career change

▶ Skills to take with you

▶ Tips on transition resumes

· ·

*I*n the 1980s, career advisers suggested changing careers to follow your dreams; in the 1990s, we write about changing careers because your career left you. As a St. Louis reader shared with me, "The least of my worries is getting stuck in my job. You should see how they cleaned house down at the brewery."

Although these words are used interchangeably in everyday conversation, technically speaking, a *job* is a position of employment within an organization; you can have lots of jobs in the same occupation. An *occupation* is your vocation, business, profession, or trade. A *career* is your entire work history. Changing careers really means changing occupations.

Changing occupations is particularly difficult for people over 50, who face a mixed job outlook with technology confiscating more jobs than it is generating. Statistics show jobs for older people growing faster than their numbers, but the growth is in low-paid service jobs, not midlevel jobs. Everywhere I turn, I see midlifers worrying about what will become of them if they step away from their life's work. Recent government data shows that, indeed, people are hanging onto their jobs — at least, those people who haven't been downsized, outplaced, or "invited" to early retirement.

Further, the economics of retirement demand that people spend more years of their lives in the workforce, especially women. We're talking today about a worklife of not 40 but 50 years or more. It's no longer an oddity to see young elders at work — a member of my office staff turned 80 on his last birthday.

In addition to necessity, a myriad of reasons exists for changing careers. They range from the desire to reestablish your enthusiasm for life or leave a lasting legacy of your time on Earth to wanting more money or a sunnier locale. Transition counselors like to say that a job is not a life sentence.

Not all career transitions happen to the over-50 crowd.

- People in their late 20s-early 30s take a look at their lives and say "Oops."
- Men and women in their late 30s-early 40s with unsatisfying careers begin to wonder if that's all there is.
- Women with grown children may hope the workplace offers salvation from terminal housecleaning.
- Military personnel are told to get out of uniform.

No matter the reason for change: Unless you want to start over at low pay from square one, learn to leverage your skills in a new direction. Bridge the future with the past.

- Career change today is fueled more by serious need than by impulsive choice. The need can be economic, or it can be because you're going braindead in your discontent. The good old days of nothing matters but following your dream are over and kaput. Vanishing good midlevel jobs is the reason.
- In changing careers, find a way to use what you know in new places; otherwise, you're a beginner competing with new graduates.
- Free your resume of jargon specific to your original occupation. If you can't learn the jargon of the new career overnight, stick to generic language.
- Compensate for your lack of experience in a new career field by showing specific crossover skills. In addition, communicate your drive, intelligence, and highest accomplishments to demonstrate swift adaptability. Bury experience irrelevant to your new target in a brief *Other Experience* section at the tail end of your resume.
- Present all your qualifications in a manner than shows their need to your prospective employer.

Portable Skills Can Turn Your Life Around

The molecules of self-discovery are elusive. You look and look, and still you miss valuable portable skills that can open new career doors. You worry that you're wasting time on this seemingly endless chore when you should be hitting the bricks to find a new career. Please don't begrudge hours and hours of time spent in self-discovery, because skills, not preferences, entitle you to be employed.

Self-discovery in a group setting is more fun than sitting alone scratching your head. Enroll in a career workshop, and you can play "My skills are bigger than your skills." The group dynamics are similar to those that motivate members in a weight-control organization: *How many pounds did you lose?* equates to *How many skills did you come up with?*

Keep in mind your portable skills message as your eyes skim the abbreviated lists of Keywords and GoodWords in Chapter 4. Plan to spend as many as 20 hours over the next few weeks in putting a name to each of your marketable skills.

For help beyond the scope of this book, see a newly revised and inexpensive 30-page booklet, *Bridging the Gap: A Learner's Guide to Transferable Skills* by Paul Breen and Urban Whitaker. This guide remains my favorite publication on the subject. The booklet is available for $6.50, postage included, from The Learning Center, P.O. Box 27616, San Francisco, CA 94127; telephone 415-873-6099. Chapter 3 has some other skills resources you can use.

The two indispensable skills for many career changers today are computer literacy and Internet access. Anyone who didn't grow up in front of a computer screen may feel a little stiff when first confronting the electronic universe. Don't cave; show Technology your superior will. Take a seminar, find a tutor, or enroll in community programs, community college, or adult education classes at a high school. Computer and Internet skills fill a resume with interview alchemy that changes your image from older and rigid to younger and flexible. Possessing these skills puts a gilt-edge to your qualifications, as employers see reduced training costs along with enhanced technological support.

If you're an under-30 career changer in need of a computer course, how did your school let you get out without knowing this stuff? Twenty-somethings are often assumed to be computer experts. Ask for a rebate from your school and then learn computers right now!

You may decide that new education will put you on the right job map. Even if you don't take a full-blown certificate, diploma, or degree program, an evening course at a local college will give you related marketable points for your resume. (As a bonus, your classmates may be professionals who have jobs in your target area, allowing you to develop new contacts.)

When you've firmly labeled your mobile marketable skills and found more than you expected (thank you, God), what's next? Here's a practical idea to begin your career shift:

Find or write job descriptions of your target occupations. If you like your current field and are leaving involuntarily because it's disappearing from under your feet, start with job descriptions in closely related jobs. Compare requirements of related jobs with your transferable skills profile. If you don't like your current field, forget I mentioned it.

To identify occupations closely related to your current field, check a library copy of the *Occupational Outlook Handbook* published by the U.S. Department of Labor.

Knowing the name of what you have to offer gets you up off your knees, out of the past, and into the future. You no longer have to say, "This is what I have done; can you use me?"

Now you can write a resume that RezReaders will respect, by saying, "This is what I can do for you that will add to your productivity, efficiency, or effectiveness. Not to mention a little bump on the bottom line."

Five KickButt Tips for Transition Resumes

If you're a career changer in transition, these tips can help smooth the ride:

1. **Choose the functional format or its hybrid offspring (described in Chapter 2).**

   This class of formats emphasizes the transferable skills in your pocket. Your presentation must help the employer see what you can do, not merely what you have done. A lockstep reverse chronological format doesn't give you the flexibility to change your image.

2. **Place the skills relevant to your intended change up front in your resume.**

   (If you don't have any, start the analysis process again or get a night job to cover your bills while you gain relevant experience or education.) Relevant skills are what RezReaders must hit on immediately. Your big message must be the first message. Everything else is in a distant second place.

3. **Take care to use appropriate headings.**

   If you are using freelance, hobby, or volunteer experience, use the heading *Work Experience* and list it first, unless you have changed your focus through education. Then begin with the heading *Education*. To refine this heading, substitute target-job related education, such as *Accounting Education* or *Healthcare Education*. Your employment history follows.

   What do you do with all the experience that was great in your old job but means zero where you want to go? Lump it together at the end of your resume under *Other Experience* or *Earlier Experience*. Shrink it to positions, titles, employers, and/or degrees and educational institutions. If extraneous experience is older than five years, squash it entirely.

   In Chapter 10, I suggest that you omit jobs that go back further than 10 to 15 years as a tactic to combat ageism without changing careers; an even shorter five-year cutoff refocuses your career direction.

4. Avoid jargon connected to your former occupation.

Jargon used in your old place makes you sound like an outsider in new career fields. Former members of the armed forces, in particular, must be careful to speak in English to avoid confusing RezReaders with military jargon. A little research in appropriate trade magazines reveals the buzzwords for your target occupation, making you sound like an insider. Whom would you hire, an outsider or an insider?

5. To follow the KickButt approach to career-transition resumes, target each position.

The help-wanted section of your major metropolitan newspaper is a convenient road map of essential functions for various jobs. An Internet search engine can direct you to resumes that others have posted in career fields of interest; compare their content with your efforts and spice up your resume as needed. Check out Chapter 1 for more on ways to research your new occupation.

Hitting Pay Dirt on Career Changing

When your job disappears or you'd like to disappear from your job, first look in the *horizontal job market* — related jobs in the same career field or related career fields. These are the areas where your transferable skills are most likely to fit and count as experience. When you cannot or will not incorporate your transferable skills into a new career field, you'll be paid as a beginner.

That's why you're wise to understand the skills-transferring process. Experiment with ways to interpret your multi-industry skills on paper — from the very first moment a RezReader sets eyes on your resume, the answers to these questions must be apparent:

Why are you qualified for the position in my company?

Why doesn't your last position relate to this one?

For more on the fine art of skills building, see my book *Cover Letters For Dummies* (IDG Books Worldwide).

Part IV
Samples of KickButt Resumes

The 5th Wave
By Rich Tennant

"Do you think I'm padding my resume by including work experience revealed in my Past Life Regression Therapy?"

In this part ...

Some things you've got to see to believe. And these resume samples have been carefully crafted so you can see different ways to handle your own KickButt effort. Your resume is really your marketing piece — make it a strong sell. You have lots of options. Be creative.

Chapter 13

A Sampling of Special Needs Resumes

- -

In This Chapter

Model resumes for

▶ New graduates

▶ Re-entry homemakers

▶ Career changers

▶ Seasoned aces

▶ People with gaps in their records

▶ College interns

▶ People with too many temporary positions

- -

*H*aving to fight for your career isn't so unusual anymore — neither are the jobwar wounds on your resume. Many who seek employment today have a few special needs marked "handle with care."

New graduates and re-entry homemakers need jobs but lack extensive paid experience. Career changers, including ex-military personnel, face the challenge of transferring skills and learning entire new job languages. Seasoned aces may have "too much" experience, and must defend themselves against labels of "overqualification." People who have gaps in their records, who were demoted down the power chain, or who were exposed to too many temporary jobs must manage their resumes to sell skills rather than experience.

The model resume samples to follow generally match the templates in Chapter 2. In some instances, the sample section headings may not match the templates exactly. The templates contain the whole shooting match of heading options so you can pick and choose the best way to market your unique needs and interests.

Gap in History

TARGETED/COMPUTER UNFRIENDLY

> Computer can't read graphic or shading; name will not retrieve. For human eyes only.

Paula G. Cramer

271 Redus Ave.
Mustang, OK 73064, (405) 123-4567

OBJECTIVE: KELLEY-KENNEDY PRINTING COMPANY PRODUCTION MANAGER
to use 12 plus years of print production management experience and graphic art knowledge

QUALIFICATIONS SUMMARY
- Handle all print project phases from design through prepress to final
- Budget management -- competent, careful
- Education (college degree plus seminars) in management backs up experience-based skills

SKILLS SUMMARY

Desktop Publishing	Staff Management
Color Separation Technology	Vendor Contract Negotiations
WP 6.0, 6.1; Lotus 123, MS Excel, Quark, Page-	Purchasing
maker, Internet, All Word Processing Software.	Blueline Approvals

ACCOMPLISHMENTS AND EXPERIENCE

> Two gaps — the first one was nearly three years, the other was six months. You have to read carefully to find the gaps because they are buried in the copy.

Lewisburg Marketing, Inc., Ada, OK
PRODUCTION MANAGER AND PRINT BUYER (Direct Mail):
Managed direct mail print production from design development through mail date for 40+
concurrent projects, meeting deadlines for 2.5 million per week, 12/94-3/98
- Directed prepress, design review, proofing, blueline approval, layout, print and
finishing schedules. Insured compliance with U.S. Postal requirements.
- Purchased for all job components and effectively managed $13 million annual budget;
price and contract copywriters, designers, and printer negotiations.

The Maupin Company, Edmond, OK
PRODUCTION COORDINATOR AND PLANNER
Planned and executed print production needs for clients, coordinated efforts of Account Executive,
Designers, and Production Staff, 4/93-6/94
- Managed estimating, purchasing, job production layout, and projects submission to graphic
design, camera and stripping, providing proofreading, scheduling, and blueline approvals,
working closely with press room manager to meet delivery deadlines.

PRIOR EXPERIENCE

Investment Litho Company, Edmond, OK
GENERAL ASSISTANT
Worked part-time throughout college. Learned printing business from master printers, 6/86-6/90

EDUCATION Bucknell University, Ada, OK - B.S. in Business and Marketing, 1989
Massbank Management Institute, Edmond, OK - 12 seminars, management

College Intern

HYBRID/COMPUTER FRIENDLY

Hard-sell language omits Chinese proficiency and is designed to counteract employer's potential assumption that Lee (in USA on student visa) will return to Asian nation. Otherwise, bilingualism should appear in objective. Using professors' names and testimonials encourages further interest.

Alexander Davidson Lee

36 W. Garnet #4   Pacific Beach, CA 92012   (619) 435-5555   E-mail: alexd.ddd@edu

Objective	**Internship or career-related summer position in Electrical Engineering;** "Highly motivated — an all-American go-getter" (says professor Bob Smith) ... "Fast-learning, earnest and hard-working graduate student" (professor Joan Roberts) ... "Smart, friendly, outgoing — real stick-to-it-iveness" (professor Tim Horrell)...

Education   San Diego State University, San Diego, CA
Degree: Masters of Science in Engineering   Major: Electrical Engineering
GPA: 3.0/4.0   Graduation: December 1998

Degree: Bachelor of Science   Major: Electrical Engineering
GPA: 3.86/4.0   Minor: Mathematics
Honors: Magna Cum Laude   Graduation: May 1997

Honors   National Dean's List, Dean's List at San Diego State University, Member of College's National Enginnering Honor Society, Member of Alpha Chi National Honor Society

Software Skills   MathCAD, MathLab, Pspice, Microcap, Fortran, Altera Logic Design System, programming M68HC11 microcontroller using Assembly language, C Language and other software utilities (word processing, spreadsheets)

Relevant Courses
- Systems, Signals and Noise
- Data Communications
- Fiber Optics Communication
- Digital Image Processing
- Random Signal Theory 1 and 2
- Transform Theory and Application
- Digital Spectral Analysis
- Communication Network Design

Includes KeyWords in skills and relevant positions

Work Experience   **Tutoring Lab Supervisor**
San Diego State University   Fall 1993-present
- Tutor students in Engineering, Mathematics, and Science courses

Assistant Engineer
Rilerad Projects Engineering, Hong Kong   Summers 1994-1997
- Collected data from engineers, produced progress reports
- Assisted bidding team, preparing documents and breakdown quotations

Administrator
National Service Hong Kong Armed Forces   March 1990-June 1993
- Scheduled military training and vocational upgrading courses
- Improved mobilization system to increase Reserve Corps processing rate during mobilization exercise

This is not a KickButt resume. What's wrong? Hint: Other than GPA, not high at master's level, where are measurements? Where are achievements? How could this resume be kicked up a couple of notches?

Activities   Vice President, Institute of Electrical and Electronic Engineers (IEEE), student chapter
Secretary of student chapter of National Society of Professional Engineers (NSPE)
Society of Physics Students
Intercultural Club
Intramural sports at San Diego State University
Fluent in Chinese

REANNA DUMON

123 Dane Street, Portland, OR 97504
(503) 456-7891
E-mail: rdumo@aol.com

Qualifications Highlights:
Seek **physical therapist position** using eight years' physical therapy and nursing experience in Canada, Switzerland, and the United States. Fluent in French, English, and Spanish. Trauma life-support, ECG, pediatrics, obstetrics, emergency and general nursing, internal medicine.

> Includes KeyWords in summary.

Education:
- Laval University, Quebec, Canada, Physical Therapy Certificate, 1996-1997
- Ste-Foy College, Ste-Foy, Quebec, Canada, D.E.C. in Technical Nursing (equivalent to RN diploma in U.S.), 1985-1988
- Garneau College, Ste-Foy, Quebec, Canada, D.E.C. in Physical Therapy, 1981-1983

Experience:

Ungava Hospital, Nunavik, Canada, 1993-1997
- Designed 25-page physical therapy clinic manual distributed to injured patients regarding methods of therapy and preventative procedures to eliminate further injury.
- Nurse: Clinical work: physical therapy, pediatric, obstetrical, and long-term follow-ups, child vaccination, laboratory procedures, home visiting, physical exams, medical evaluations, multidisciplinary case discussions.
    Community Health: school vaccination programs.
    Administration: patient transfers, medical visits, arranging meetings.

> Includes KeyWords in job descriptions.

Ungava Hospital, Nunavik, Canada, 1991-1993
- Coordinated physical therapy schedule and program for 16 patients.
- Pediatrics, obstetrics, general medicine nurse. Monitored staff of 30 pediatric nurses; managed 57 patients.
- Coordinated schedule for 37 nurses in general medicine unit, maximizing hospital efficiency in patient care and personal organizational skills.

Canntonnal Hospital of Fribourg, Fribourg, Switzerland, 1990-1991
- Nurse, Department of Internal Medicine. Managed 26 patients, 8 with PT needs.
- Trained 11 interns on internal medicine procedures, enhancing leadership, management, and interpersonal skills to implement team-work ideal of hospital.

> Gives results.

Bassee-Nord Health Center, Quebec, Canada, 1988-1990
- Performed daily physical therapy sessions with 13 pediatric patients.
- Head Nurse — emergency care, general medicine and pediatrics nurse.
- Promoted to Head Nurse in emergency-care unit within first eight months.
- Supervised 23 nursing interns and coordinated medicine schedules for 35 patients.

> Because physical therapy, not nursing, is goal, Dumon leads with physical therapy experience, although nursing experience is dominant. Dumon moves in and out of the two professions -- PT and nursing.

Romero Cortez
42 Plains Road
Mystic, CT 06493
(203) 555-6932
E-mail: romeroc@drd.sfi.com

Senior Creative/Marketing Executive
Experienced in major account management, new product and strategic concept development, advertising and promotion; spearheaded revenue growth from $13 million to $180 million in 5 years.

Omits section headings for more direct impact.

- Increased one company's value from $50 million to sales price of $225 million
- Revitalized company by effecting $10 million sales increase

Effective leader skilled in building, training-and-motivating highly profitable creative teams and directing major projects to completion on time with strong cost control. Track record of developing and maintaining corporate relationships.

Creative/Marketing Success Highlights

"Advertises" marketing achievements.

Marketing Theme	Client
Tannik's Capitalist Tool	Tannik's Magazine
Call them with clarity	RTO Telephones
Fly us	Abroad Airlines
Oil No More	Oil Gleaners Inc.
Let Our Machines Work, You Think	Mattison Products
Feel sensitive	Crimson Skin Products
Every Bit Crystal Quality	Crystal Diskettes
Moist and Flavorful Food	New-Taste Dog Food

Awards
Clio, American Institute of Graphic Arts, Rissoli Award, Best Read Ad-Rosser Reeves, Communications Arts Award, Outdoor Billboard Design Award, and Andy Award, International Film Festival Silver Medal, Connecticut Art Directors Club Gold Medal

(1 of 2)

Can change to computer friendly by switching "Creative Marketing Success Highlights" with "Professional Experience." That's the order in which computers expect to find data. But for human viewing, current presentation is different and effective.

Romero Cortez

Developed all RTO-TV Network advertising for 2 years. Directed turn-around of Morning brand cereal division. Other creative assignments in advertising, direct marketing and new product development launches for:

Generative Appliances	American Bottling Co.
International Athletics Association	New Foods
Sweet Candy Company	Crystal

Sells industry reputation before employment history.

Professional Experience

Vice President,
Creative Director
Wilton Marketing & Communications, Wilton, CT
1989-Present

Vice President,
Associate Creative Director
McConnell and McCarthy, Inc., Manhattan, NY
1986-1989

Vice President,
Associate Creative Director
Mark Jenkins Company Advertising, Inc., Manhattan, NY
1979-1986

Romero Cortez shows he's a pro by using advertising skills on his resume -- in this model, Cortez makes a virtue of open white space, citing only a few standout achievements.

(2 of 2)

Seasoned Ace
ACCOMPLISHMENT/COMPUTER FRIENDLY

Dana M. Brigham
123 Teal Way, Tujunga, CA 91042, (714) 222-4985
e-mail: dbrigham@infonet.com

Urban Planner: 15 years' experience in urban planning with substantial management experience in public and private sectors. Experienced in preparing and managing: general plan revisions; zoning code administration; redevelopment plans; environmental projects.

Different typeface than body text for more attention.

Qualifications and Accomplishments:
- Planner for city of Laguna Niguel, managing review of large-scale urban projects.

- Managed general plan preparation for Irvine, Palmdale, and San Jose including environmental analysis of plans' impacts, surviving court challenge.

Gives results.

- Supervised zoning section of Irvine Planning Department for over four years, developing commission agenda and preparing staff reports to commission and City Council.

- Supervised 37 planners in public sector for Irvine, Palmdale, and San Jose.

Brigham departs from template by combining qualifications and accomplishments.

- Assisted in establishing plan in Palmdale immediately following its incorporation.

- Directed task force in designing and implementing new hillside grading/development standards for Palmdale, developing builder sensitivity to community goals.

- Organized Hillside Development Panel for 1995 American Planning Association

- Managed preparation of East Santa Monica Boulevard Strategic Plan and East Irvine Specific Plan for Pasadena; coordinated with 56 planners, presented to large groups.

Employment:
CITY OF IRVINE, Irvine, California, 1996-Present
Special Projects Planner, Planning and Community Development Department.

Maximizes white space.

LOCKEN AND CO., Santa Monica, California, 1993-1996
Director of Planning Department.

CITY OF PALMDALE, Palmdale, California, 1989-1993
Senior Project Manager, Planning and Research Section.

KLO ASSOCIATES, Palmdale, California, 1987-1989
Senior project manager of preparing environmental impact reports.

WOLHBAHN & SONS, Santa Monica, California, 1985-1987
Senior Planning Consultant providing advisory services to local municipalities.

CITY OF SAN JOSE, San Jose, California, 1981-1985
Supervising Associate Planner, Zoning Division, Planning Department.

Education:
Bachelor of Arts, Political Science, University of Sacramento, Sacramento, California, 1980
Master of Science, Public Administration, California State University, Sacramento, California 1983

Professional Affiliations:
American Planning Association, American Institute of Certified Planners

Seasoned Ace
ACCOMPLISHMENT/COMPUTER FRIENDLY

Older human resource pro wishes to re-enter private sector after government stint; limits work history to 10 years.

ANDREW WALLACE
P.O. BOX 123 NEWPORT, LONG ISLAND, NY 11413
(212) 456-1997
awall@aol.com

**Human Resource position using recruitment, appraisal
and benefit skills, accumulated over 10 years**

QUALIFICATIONS:

➤ Directed human resource systems for two mid-sized corporations
➤ Worked inside EEOC structure; bullet-proof employee management
➤ Expert in recruiting, benefits, evaluations, training, and outplacement
➤ Use computer -- or manual -- applicant/employee tracking systems
➤ Can manage contingent workforce

ACCOMPLISHMENTS:

➤ Investigated and negotiated resolutions of 400 allegations of employment discrimination. Led investigation teams and instructed on negotiation procedures to maximize resolution success.

➤ Performed EEO consultation, trained more than 60 employer and university organizations in human resource skills to establish increasingly effective management-staff working relationship.

➤ Received 12 annual merit-based promotions; managed staff of 15 recruiters.

RECENT PROFESSIONAL EXPERIENCE:

➤ 11/94 to 12/97 -- **Employment Equality Commission, New York,** NY -- Federal Investigator
➤ 9/93 to 6/97 -- **University Of New York City, Queens,** NY -- Adjunct Faculty
➤ 11/93 to 11/94 -- **Swanky Interiors, New York,** NY -- Human Resources Director
➤ 6/87 to 9/93 -- **Lucrative Corporation, Buffalo,** NY -- Human Resources Manager

EDUCATION:

➤ **Central New York University** -- Master of Sciences, Human Resource Administration
➤ **Mariner College** -- Bachelor of Arts, Management of Human Resources
➤ **New York College of Law** -- Continuing coursework towards Juris Doctor degree

PROFESSIONAL ASSOCIATIONS:

➤ Human Resource Association of New York
➤ Society for Human Resource Management
➤ American Society of Training & Development
➤ American Bar Association Student Division
➤ State Bar of New York Student Division
➤ Kiwanis International

New Graduate

REVERSE CHRONOLOGICAL & TARGETED/COMPUTER FRIENDLY

> Lutwig's research on the target showed they wanted an energetic young person with his degrees. Objective and education centered for formal look and to highlight degrees target hirer favors.

DALE K. LUTWIG

12 West 34th Street , Los Angeles, CA 11121
(213) 567-8910   E-mail: twig@nnn.gov

Objective : CONGRESSIONAL AIDE

JURIS DOCTOR INTERNATIONAL LEGAL STUDIES
Occidental University, College of Law 1997

MASTER OF ARTS, POLITICAL SCIENCE
Adele School of Citizenship and Public Affairs 1994
Concentration in Government Planning & International Negotiation
Teaching Assistant in International Negotiation

BACHELOR OF ARTS, POLITICS AND SOCIOLOGY
University of California, Los Angeles 1993, Dean's List

Bar Admission: CA and NJ Passed entrance examinations. Admissions pending.

> Summary omitted for cover letter.

WORK EXPERIENCE

1995-1996   **Office of the United States Trade Representative**
Assisted Deputy Assistant US Trade Representative in analyzing House and Senate bills. Reconstructed 25 legislative provisions which complicated international trade obligations. Corresponded with corporations, trade associations, congressional staff members and other Federal agencies. Developed working closely with international negotiations. Trade representative John Katan compliments my work: "Best intern we have."

> Complimentary quotes accentuate skills and promise.

1994   **Los Angeles Department of Consumer Affairs**
Assisted investigators in enforcing Attorney General's Guidelines for Fair Advertising. Accumulated strong background in advertising ethics proceedings.

1993   **Charles Swabb**
Assisted 19 account executives in management activities, including investor research, telemarketing, mass mailings, computerized clerical operations and communications. Tremendous experience with intercompany and public communications. Praised for follow-through and organization (office manager Tom Cannon).

1990-1993   **Reese, Riley & Thorne**
Assisted library staff, paralegals, and attorneys with all library functions, including organization and research. Modernized 14 computers. Compiled legal information for 32 lawsuits from cases and articles, acquiring early experience with legal negotiations.

MISCELLANEOUS

> Technical skills detailed to target employer's needs.

- Proficient with all applications, including LEXIS/NEXIS/WESTLAW data bases.
- Hobbies include sailboat racing and golf.

> Personal interest included; Lutwig's research shows target company's RezReaders value interest in sports.

New Graduate
LINEAR/COMPUTER FRIENDLY

> Grades speak for themselves. Testimonial backs up claim of favorable faculty comments.

Herman Ling

123 Northrop Avenue #4 Ft. Lauderdale, Florida 33308
(305) 566-6789   E-mail: hling@jkuafu.edu

Objective Marketing position in Agribusiness or Chemicals

Qualifications Focus: plant pathology. MBA/Master's in Plant Pathology/ agriculture undergraduate degree. Two years' international marketing experience. Bilingual — Chinese and English. Computer literate. Rated tops by grades and favorable faculty comments in graduate studies: ("Herman Ling is the most industrious student to come through here in several years" — U. of Colorado marketing professor Karl Weber.)

Communications Skills
- Computer: MS Word, Excel, Powerpoint, WordPerfect, Lotus 123, Freelance, Harvard Graphics, PSI-Plot, SAS JUMP, QBasic programming, and main frame
- Language: Chinese (Mandarin and several dialects)

> Gives details on bilingual and computer claims in summary.

Experience

8/94-7/97 **Graduate Research Assistant**
University of Colorado, Department of Plant Pathology, Boulder, CO
- Designed and implemented experiments in greenhouse, growth chamber, and field
- Developed weather-based advisory for improving control of plant disease with reduced fungicide

7/92-8/94 **Account Manager, Department of Marketing and Sales**
Detect Bio-Pharmacy Group, Beijing, PR China
- Developed channel strategies for entering Chinese marketplace
- Managed and developed sales accounts
- Developed promotion plan for marketing new medicine
- Participated in joint venture for manufacturing ingredients

> Prior experience in China. This experience is for U.S. job, thus quote from U.S. professor; for a job in China, would emphasize China connections.

9/89-6/92 **Social Coordinator, Department Student Association;**
Co-editor, Department Student Journal
Beijing Agricultural University, Beijing, PR China

Education **Master of Business Administration,** 1999, GPA 4.0/4.0
University of Miami, Miami, FL

Master of Science, Plant Pathology, 1997, GPA 3.8/4.0
University of Colorado, Boulder, Boulder, CO

Bachelor of Science, Plant Protection, 1992, GPA (comparable) 4.0/4.0
Beijing Agricultural University, Beijing, People's Republic of China

Publications **Ling, Herman,** Grant, P., and Milton, F. 1998 "Effects of precipitation and temperature on garden crop infection." *Plant Disease.*

Ling, Herman, and Kilkenny, E. 1998 "Comparison of weather-dependent crops based on soil concentration." *Plant Disease.*

Activities American Phytopathological Society

> Despite advanced degrees, placed experience first to show market orientation.

Re-Entry Homemaker
REVERSE CHRONOLOGICAL/COMPUTER FRIENDLY

Faith Marks

167 Vanderbilt Road
Harrisburg, PA 12101

(916) 779-1434
E-mail: fmarks@cts.com

Space between text and line.

Objective
Social Studies Teacher, grades 5-12
Teaching is my life. Comfortable with computers, daily communication, and research via e-mail and the Internet. Computer focus promises that children taught will not be left behind in a competitive era.

Objective mixed with summary: concentration on e-mail & Internet shows stay-at-home is up-to-date.

Education
Bachelor of Science in Secondary Education
Pennsylvania State University, 1995

Pennsylvania Teaching Credential:
Economics, Geography, United States and
World History, Grades 5-12

Honors
• National Dean's List, 1994
• Alpha Lambda, 1992, Freshman Honor Society
• Phi Eta Sigma, 1992, Freshman Honor Society

Fast-learning, willingness to put self-interest aside for team good.

Teaching Experience

Substitute Teacher, Townville Elementary School   Fall 1995
• Became expert at instant lesson plan preparation. Never refused last-minute assignments
• Worked with diverse student groups, expanding range of teaching capabilities. Not intimidated by challenge of middle-school behavioral problems
• Used considerable experience with children, ages five-twelve. Created exciting and motivational lesson plans. Principal Morgan Rathbone says "Faith Marks gives 110% to her substitute teaching assignments. Her students get energized by her classroom technique. I only wish we had a staff opening. I'd hire her in a second! "

Complimentary quote used to explain why she was not hired here if she's so great.

Student Teacher, Townville Middle School, 10 weeks   Spring 1995
Grant Middle School, 6 weeks
• Taught US History, Geography, and Government; developed multi-faceted daily lesson plans for each course
• Perfected computer fluency. Strengthened supervisory roles, delegation ability, organizational skills and motivational techniques. Worked full-time while parenting
• Instructed extracurricular activities, including softball and computer club

Additional Experience
Advised graduate students, worked as student financial aid liaison. Analyzed student financial information and matched to available funding

Seasoned Ace
LINEAR/COMPUTER FRIENDLY

> Alternative heading for Objective.

Lee Ralston

7702 Ridge Road   **Tacoma, Washington 90543**
(206) 555-9876   **E-mail: lralst@aol.com**

Profile: Property Management professional seeks to use high-quality history in supervisory position. More than 15 years' solid experience A to Z in property management.

> Quantifies achievements.

Qualifications:
- Skilled in profit & loss, reductions, distribution, and financial administration
- Restructure marketing plans strategically, advancing returns in excess of 20%
- Record of enthusiastic achievement of corporate objectives
- LIHTC (tax credit), Bond, Section 8, HODAG, New Construction and Renovations
- Managed multi-family properties in Washington, California, Oregon, Arizona, Colorado, and Utah

> Ampersand OK — familiar phrase.

> KeyWords throughout.

Education and Training:
- **Bachelor of Arts in Education,** University of Puget Sound, Tacoma, Washington
- **College of Certified Property Managers,** Apartment Management, Real Estate Finances and Management

Designations:
- Certified Apartment Property Supervisor
- Washington Real Estate License

> White space and bullets improve readability.

Professional Experience:

1993-Present   **Senior Asset Manager**   Greengrove Point Properties, Inc.

> Quantifies and gives results of achievements.

- Manage marketing and operations programs for over 2,000 units.
- Recruit, train, and hire over 100 employees, maximizing $2M in capital improvements.
- Consult on all EEOC and fair housing issues, minimizing legal consultation costs by $2,000.

1992-1993   **Regional Manager**   Builder Companies of Washington

- Facilitated marketing programs for 10-12 properties throughout Washington.
- Superintended successful lease-up and operation of 23 story luxury hi-rise property in Seattle.
- Directed $2 million renovation of 25 year old property on coast of Washington.

1990-1992   **District Manager**   Washington Property Management

- Created marketing and operations programs for two properties in Tacoma, WA.
- Facilitated $2 million renovation with lease-up three months ahead of schedule.
- Maintained 98% occupancy in New Construction lease.

> Ampersand OK — company name.

1985-1990   **Area Manager**   Benedict, Young, Dalton, & McMillan

Assistant Manager on 1672 unit property in Seattle, Washington.
- Led company nationally for two years in leasing, averaging over 120 new leases per month.
- Portfolio consisted of 2,000 units and over 100 employees.
- Directed monthly regional sales meetings, initiated energy savings program that accomplished $150,000 work done to 14 properties with profit exceeding $12,000.

Grouping Temporary Jobs
ACCOMPLISHMENT/COMPUTER FRIENDLY

BETH SHELTON

1849 Warner Road, Newark, Delaware 19905   Phone: (302) 555-6778
                                                                 E-mail: shelton@khl.com

Objective

Position as **Administrative Assistant/Executive Secretary** — using detail-oriented skills and experience accumulated over 9 years

Qualifications

- More than 10 years' secretarial/administrative experience; keyboard speed of 90 wpm
- Proficient in Microsoft Word, WordPerfect, Windows, Lotus, Excel, FileMaker Pro

Accomplishments

- Responded promptly to technical requests from Parker clients (account average: $25,000), advising on hardware and software issues, ensuring client satisfaction

- Supported office operations of 35-bed hospital ward; developed substantial ability to prioritize duties and service large numbers of people in high-pressure environment

- Researched, compiled and prepared crucial data, independently and with little supervision — developing strong self-management skills

- Organized meetings and workshops, arranged travel for conferences averaging 20 executives; as noted by Tom Rogers, corporate vice president: "Beth fits together all the cogs and wheels here; without her, it's chaos."

- Tracked 250 medical admissions, discharges, and transfers on computer

- Resolved issues after hours and on weekends, meeting challenges with commitment

Job History

Combined temporary jobs under one heading to avoid looking like job hopper.

Administrative Assistant and Secretary, Hammond Temporaries, Dover, Del.   1994-Present
Assistant Database Manager, Parker Regional Medical Systems, Newark, Del.   1991-1994
Assistant Office Manager, Hyde Transport Company, Dover, Del.   1989-1991
Secretary to Computing Manager, Range Systems, Newark, Del.   1982-1989

Education

Bachelor of Arts in Business Management, 3.8/4.0 GPA   Awarded 1998
Newark College, Newark, Del.

Seasoned Ace
KEYWORD & LINEAR/COMPUTER FRIENDLY

Objective woven into KeyWord summary.

Griffin T. Stenner
2345 Fremont Blvd.   Santa Fe, NM 87501
(505) 555-0006   Messages taken at (505) 333-8000
E-Mail: griffsten@aol.com

Senior-level sales and distribution management position

12 years' experience in supervisory positions. Sales and distribution experience. Budgeting. Profit & loss responsibility. Customer service. Materials and product management. Employee selection and training. Strategic and tactical planning. Marketing. Facility location. Product training. Labor relations. Manufacturing plant management. Computerized environment and pricing.

Business Experience

Divides jobs by titles, highlighting upward mobility over long period with single employer.

1984-Present DUNCAN TRANSIT COMPANY, Santa Fe, New Mexico
1994-Present **Director of Aftermarket Business**

Amper-sand OK here — familiar phrase.

Profit & loss responsibility for $40 million aftermarket parts division. Supervise 16 sales and 35 distribution staff for sales, marketing, materials management, customer service, distribution and product management. Serve on Executive Committee for policy making and strategizing
• Facilitated strategic plan increasing sales 30%, exceeding 25% assets return
• Chaired integrated software system committee
• Edited sales literature and media campaign for $3 million retail expansion
• Sharpened inventory accuracy to 97.5% with new bar code system, significantly reducing manufacturing downtime

1990-1995   **Corporate Distribution Manager**
Managed warehouse, distribution and traffic functions for two locations of more than 10,000 stock-keeping units. Assumed plant responsibility for distribution of product to 860 retail stores weekly.
• Designed and relocated new distribution center on schedule and $200,000 under budget
• Received **Star of the Year** award from employer for product quality and distribution service levels
• Lowered total distribution cost 24%, saving $1.8M over five years

1984-1990   **Account Manager**
Developed first- and second-level distribution and manufacturing accounts in 30 key market areas, while maintaining in excess of 40 existing accounts in eight states. Conducted sales, product, and technical meetings for distributorship managers and sales staff.
• Top company salesperson in 1985, 1986, and 1988
• Increased sales by 220% to $4.4M in two years

Achievement numbers combined for over one year to show high–impact results.

Education

No years given.

Bachelor of Science, Business Administration, University of New Mexico, Santa Fe
Senior Executive Management Course, Santa Fe Community College, New Mexico

Military/Career Changer
FUNCTIONAL/COMPUTER FRIENDLY

Franklin S. Tower
842 Harvest Dr.
Philadelphia, PA 19103
(215) 911-9409
stower@prodigy.com

Mechanical Engineer

12 years' experience in mechanical engineering with a diverse background in design and engineering contract management.

PROFESSIONAL EXPERIENCE AND ACCOMPLISHMENTS

Mechanical Design
- Designed laboratory expansion for waste treatment plant. Upgraded underground storage tanks to meet EPA standards which also resulted in a 65% increase in treatment and storage efficiency.

- Improved design of fire training pit, including redesign of pump and pipe sizing and oil/water separator selection. Redesign allowed substantial increase in control of flow direction and water pressure.

- Designed recirculation system for waste treatment plant trickling filter which decreased water usage by 18% and filter replacement rate.

- Developed design for electrical contacts for a major electrical connector manufacturer on a contractual basis. New design improved materials usage and improved production time by 5%.

Engineering Contract Management
- Evaluated drafting and engineering sections' performance, quality, and compliance with specified contract, scheduling and ensuring time tables for production. Consistently led teams in finishing projects ahead of schedule.

- Rewrote performance specifications to improve bonus incentive. Eliminated unrelated requirements in bonus program, resulting in 15% increase in worker efficiency.

- Evaluated contractors for compliance with EPA and safety regulations affirming environmental responsibility and decreasing worker down time due to accidents.

- Implemented priority-setting program that decreased project and production redundancy over a five-year period.

General Management
- Supervised buildings and ground maintenance and repair shops. Duties included review and approval of project schedules, quality inspection of work

> Converts military jargon into civilian terms.

(1 of 2)

Franklin S. Tower

in progress and completed work, coordination of requirements between sections, briefing of senior supervisors. Developed rotating maintenance schedule that improved efficiency 20% and eliminated redundant work requests.

- Supervised new office that was created to ease difficulties in closing Air Force Base engineering section. Implemented programs to track location and disposal of supplies and materials resulting in better-than-forecast inventory elimination. Developed and implemented procedures and outplacement programs that ensured meeting the closing deadline and placed 46% of former federal employees in private sector positions.

Demonstrates concern for people, not just products.

- Managed aircraft maintenance and repair branches with 475 employees and 15 shops. Monitored maintenance in progress and briefed senior supervisors on maintenance scheduling. Wrote performance reviews and performed counseling for at-risk personnel, resulting in 12% decrease in worker turn-around.

EMPLOYMENT HISTORY

1986-present, Officer, United States Air Force
5/86-11/86, Mechanical Drafter, Frankish Design Company, Langston,TX

By not specifying rank:
1. downplays lack of advancement while in military service, and
2. moderates civilian anxiety of military rank.

EDUCATION

- Bachelor of Science in Mechanical Engineering,
  California Polytechnic University, San Luis Obispo, 1986

- Officers Training School, 1988

(2 of 2)

Chapter 14

A Sampling of KickButt Resumes

· ·

In This Chapter

Model resumes in 12 career fields

▶ Chemistry

▶ Computer graphic design

▶ Editing

▶ Financial management

▶ Health club management

▶ Nonprofit management

▶ Public relations

▶ Real estate

▶ Restaurant management

▶ Retail management

▶ Sales

▶ Speech-language pathology

· ·

*P*repare to meet the first blackbelt graduates of KickButt boot camp, from entry- to management-level job seekers. Real people wrote the originals of these resumes, but we (my staff and I) tore them up and rewrote them to meet KickButt standards. All names and contact information are fictional, but the raw selling power behind every one is real.

Although KickButt formats (illustrated by the templates in Chapter 2) are mercilessly sell-hungry, they are by no means rigid — not every section heading works for every resume. Choose your section headings to flaunt your best moves.

In the interest of not chopping trees, we chopped material — that is, some resumes to follow would have been two pages had we not eliminated text. Occasionally, as another conservation measure, we used ampersands (&) to replace the word "and." Should you use ampersands on your own resume? Yes, but very gingerly. Ampersands are okay for

- Company names
- Copyrights
- Logos
- Familiar phrases — "P & L Statements."

Otherwise, spell out the word "and."

Here is a selection of KickButt model resumes.

Assistant Retail Manager
ACCOMPLISHMENT/COMPUTER UNFRIENDLY

Jack Straw

2424 Heavensent Lane, Wichita, Kansas 67056   (316) 446-5513   E-mail: jstraw@aol.com

OBJECTIVE

Position as **assistant retail manager** using my eight years of experience in retail, technical sales and software experience.

SUMMARY

- Hard-won and successful experience in many aspects of retailing: sales, marketing, operations, training and service.

- Can open and manage retail software and other technical products. Qualified as assistant manager of retail store; qualified as department manager of superstore. Managed new retail location ranking in top ten of 64 stores within first year.

> Web merchandising is hot buzzword in late '90's; "start-up study" means Straw studied topic, is ready to implement new selling technology for new employer.

- Internet/World Wide Web merchandising start-up study.

HIGHLIGHTS OF SKILLS

- Opening, operating **new locations**
- **Growing sales:** make **customer-first**
- **Budgeting, extending credit**
- **Recruiting** and interviewing
- **Training** and retraining staff
- **Telemarketing**
- Product display
- Promotion, advertising strategies
- **Software licensing, electronics, purchasing**

- All major **point-of-sale equipment**
- **Computer skills:** PCs and Macs; General Store, Excel, Lotus 1-2-3, QuickBooks, Aldus Pagemaker, CAD, CorelDraw, Desktop Publisher, Superpaint, Windows Office including Word.
- **Internet skills:** World Wide Web, e-mail, FTP

> Can be made computer friendly by eliminating vertical design lines.

PROFESSIONAL EXPERIENCE

Video Tape Tub, La Costa, KS -- Customer Rep   1996-Present
Customer service, product display, inventory maintenance, video rentals and returns. "Best help I've had in five years" (Owner Cal Showers).

Custom Names, Delmar, KS -- Consumer Service Representative   1995
Extensive retail sales and technical support for software, computer equipment, satellite TV, electronics and home theater equipment. Maintained average monthly sales of $30,000, ranking fourth in sales. Heavy telemarketing component.

(1 of 2)

Jack Straw

The Cutting Edge, Rancho, KS -- Assistant Manager   1993-1995
Serviced upscale clientele in high-end software, electronics and video game retail store. Handled sales, purchasing, staff training, work schedules, product inventory and display, technical support for electronics and software, bank deposits and staff management.

Software Bug, Carlsbad, KS -- Night Manager   1990-1993
Evening management of software retail store. Innovative sales strategies brought store from 47th in sales ranking to 8th in a 64-store chain. Other work: employee recruiting and dismissal, training, retraining, scheduling, staff management, technical support. Awarded Employee of Month four separate months.

Temp-a-Medic, La Jolla, CA -- Healthcare Staffer   1989-1990
Matched healthcare temps with hospitals in Los Angeles and San Diego. Developed organizational skills, calm resilience when chaos threatened and acceptance of high-pressure, detail-reliant environment. Sold new accounts at seven hospitals.

EDUCATION

62 academic hours toward bachelor's degree; have kept nose to grindstone taking 3-6 hours per semester for past five years. Anticipate testing out of 18 hours; expect degree June, 2001.

VOLUNTEER AND PERSONAL EXPERIENCE

-- Coach, Roller Hockey Little League of North County. Coached winning North (San Diego) County team of more than 30 youths, ages 7-12. Grateful for opportunity to develop strong interpersonal, cross-generational, cross-cultural and community networks. Proven talent with teamwork, organization, people of various economic classes.

-- Interests include computers, electronics, ice hockey, computer drafting and freehand illustration.

> Straw's goal is completion of college degree. To indicate intent to enroll for more than 3 to 6 hours per semester while working in retailing, noted for long hours, would be risky.

(2 of 2)

Chemist
PROFESSIONAL/COMPUTER FRIENDLY

Dixon Marbend
123 Moon Road, Flanders, New Jersey 07836   (201) 584-0150

Chemist ◄—— *Objective replaced with job title, summary follows -- personalizes the format.*

Six years' research experience with increasing responsibility and successful record of instrumentation and scientific achievement. Specialty: Silicon. Designed computer systems (mainframe to micro) for laboratory instrument automation, including patented design. Published presenter.

EDUCATION

- Ph.D., Chemical Design & Engineering, University of Rochester, Rochester, New York
  Dissertation: Manipulation of Luminescent Porous Silicon Structures
- Master of Science, Chemistry, University of Rochester, Rochester, New York
- Bachelor of Science, Physics, Honors, University of New Jersey-Elizabeth, New Jersey

EXPERIENCE AND ACCOMPLISHMENTS

Quantifies achievements and responsibilities.

1993-1995   **Research Assistant, University of Rochester, Rochester, N.Y.**
- Patented procedure for "Engineering of Luminescent Images on Silicon" and coauthored seven publications (see addendum).
- Conducted research investigations of luminescent silicon and spearheaded procedure for fabricating structures with photoelectricity; managed staff of 5 assistants.
- Delivered 14 presentations of results and research in progress to professors in department.
- Tutored 37 undergraduates in research and chemistry theory, increasing teaching skills.
- Purchased $79,000 in chemicals and equipment for starting research lab.

Shows results of achievements.

1992-1993   **Research Assistant, University of New York, New York City** ◄——
- Built non-vibrating 1.5 ton aluminum platform for NMR management.
- Assisted professor with construction of super-conducting NMR spectrometer.
- Designed and manufactured integrated circuits in lab.

Minimizes less relevant jobs.

1992   **Research Assistant, University of New Jersey-Elizabeth, Elizabeth, N.J.**
- Investigated methods for feature distortion in scanning tunneling microscopy.

1991-1992   **Laboratory Assistant, University of New York, New York City**
- Prepared and maintained delicate equipment and chemicals for chemistry labs, ensuring maximum performance and efficiency.
- Worked with 57 teacher assistants and students, developing training skills.

Skills section added to format, enhancing abilities and using more KeyWords.

TECHNICAL SKILLS

Steady state photoluminescence	Machining aluminum and Plexiglas
Raman, FTIR, and UV-Vis spectroscopy	Macintosh: Word, KaleidaGraph,
Inert atmosphere (Schlenk and dry box)	Canvas, Aldus PageMaker, MacDraw,
Standard electrochemistry/photochemistry	Hypercard, Chem 3D, Excel, Internet
AFM, STM, and SEM	

(1 of 2)

Dixon Marbend **(201) 584-0150**

PUBLICATIONS

"Engineering of Luminescent Images on Silicon." Marbend, U.S. Patent No. 1,234,567; Jan 1, 1997

"Silicon Technology." Saynor and Marbend in 1997 *Martin-Marietta Yearbook of Science Technology*; Martin-Marietta: New York, N.Y. 1996, 123-4

"Optical Cavities in Silicon Film." Saynor, Curbin, and Marbend in *Electrochemic Journal,* 1996, 21

"Emission from Etched Silicon." Marbend and Piner in *Material Research Symposium,* 1996, 12, 3456-7

"Color Image Generation on Silicon." Marbend and Saynor in *Chemical Science,* 1995, 123, 4567-8

"Porous Silicon Micro-Dension." Marbend and Saynor in *Physics Applied,* 1995, 45, 678-9

"Stoichiometric Cadmium Electrodeposition." Krass and Marbend, *MaterialChem,* 1994, 1, 23

HONORS, MEMBERSHIPS & PRESENTATIONS

Chemical Symposium Research Fellow, Undergraduate Honors Fellows, Winter Research Fellow

Chemical Symposium, Chemical Alliance, Electrochemistry Association

Marbend, Saynor and Curbin. *Emission from Etched Silicon.* Presented at 123rd Chemical Symposium, Detroit, Michigan, January 1996

Marbend. *Porous Silicon Micro-Dension.* Presented at 234th Chemical Alliance, New York City, New York, January 1995

> New scanning software reads italics; old ones do not. Marbend telephoned RezReader to determine scanning software. When old programs are used, Marbend substitutes a second version of his resume, replacing italics with quotes around same typeface used in rest of resume.

Health Club Manager
REVERSE CHRONOLOGICAL/COMPUTER FRIENDLY

Hilda Larson
347 Appleview Drive, Chicago, IL 60611
(312) 555-9876

*** CONFIDENTIAL ***
Work (brief messages only) (312) 555-9876

> Larson leads with graduate degree because health clubs are subject to legal liability for client injuries, aggravated by employees without formal credentials.

> Larson's boss doesn't know she's job-hunting; note "Confidential" and work telephone number with mention to keep calls to arrangement-making only.

Objective and Qualifications:

Health and Fitness Industry Management: Master's and undergraduate degree in Health and Fitness. Eight years' individual and group health education and exercise leadership. Extensive background in equestrian skills, dance, gymnastics, martial arts, swimming, and strength work. Use wellness and preventive-medicine techniques.

Professional Experience:

5/94-Present University of Chicago Center for Disease Research & Health, Chicago, IL
- **Health Promotion Specialist, Researcher, Exercise Physiologist**
Provide monthly nutrition testing and counseling to 120 individuals, 300 in group. Conduct health and fitness classes -- 350 per month. Organization and promotion skills recognized with selection for Health Promotion Coordinator to Chicago Executive Program.

10/92-5/94 Wheaton College Health and Fitness, Wheaton, IL
- **Instructor and Program Consultant**
Produced bimonthly newsletter, wellness counseling, and campus-wide publicity, leading to 25% membership increase in health and fitness club in 3 months.

11/92-5/94 Fitness Plus Enterprises, Inc., Winnetka, IL
- **Personal Fitness Trainer, Group Exercise Instructor**
Taught group exercise classes and designed personal fitness programs for 550 individual clients. Popular trainer among special groups (disabled and elderly).

5/92-7/92 Aerobics Activity Center, Winnetka, IL
- **Assistant to the Associate Director**
Designed activity program, teaching, lecturing, and performing market research.

9/91-5/92 University of Chicago, Chicago, IL
- **Graduate Teaching Fellow**
Designed and taught. Advised 24 independent study projects for undergraduate students. Wrote two proposals to Health/Fitness Department Chair, initiating development of new graduate instruction program; result $5,000 grant from school.

(1 of 2)

Hilda Larson

(312) 555-9876

Education:

Master of Health Science, Health Education Concentration, University of Chicago, 1993
Bachelor of Science, Honors, Kinesiology, Adult Fitness Concentration, University of Chicago, 1989
Guest Scholar, Physical Education Professional Division, University of Chicago, Winter and Spring 1992

> It's OK to list the education section on the 2nd page because Larson refers to it in the qualifications section.

Certifications:

1996	Exer-Safety Associates Step/Bench Certification
1994	American College of Sports Medicine Health and Fitness Instructor
1993	American Council on Exercise Certified Personal Trainer

Presentations:

- University of Chicago Executive Program, Summer 1996 and 1997
- Sport Cardiologists and Nutritionist National Conference, Spring 1993
- Buen Salud Annual Gathering, Mexico City, Mexico, Spring 1993
- University of Chicago Individual Fitness Design, Fall 1992

Conferences:

- World Fitness IDEA International Conference, Las Vegas, NV, 1997
- IDEA Personal Trainer's Conference, San Jose, CA, 1996
- Regional Northeast Wellness Conference, Boston, MA, 1993

Awards and Honors:

- Academic Honors, University of Chicago, 1986 and 1987
- Harriet Wilson Award for Kindness and Receptivity to Others, 1984
- Cross Cultural Awareness Award for Achievement in Cross Cultural Skills, 1984
- Varsity Letters in Dance and Gymnastics, University of Chicago, 1984
- Honored as "Outstanding in public relations and efficiency," 1990
- National Amateur Champion at the National Horse, Madison Square Garden 1984

> Despite national standing in equestrian skills, urban health clubs aren't known for horse stables, thus award is placed last. Yet such a prominent skill can't be omitted -- further, RezReader may be a rider and identify with Larson.

(2 of 2)

Public Relations Representative
REVERSE CHRONOLOGICAL/COMPUTER FRIENDLY

Lorna Quito
Roßmarket 12, 12345 Frankfurt/Main, 12-8907-87, Germany
Telephone 2323-90000
E-mail: lquito@gold.com.de

Objective

Communications or public relations position, using high-stakes skills: writing, editing, placement, promotion, speaking, production, and Web page design. Employ all media: newspaper, magazines, radio, television, multimedia, online. ← Note: Larger type for summary hook.

Employment

1995-Present   **Publicist**, European Red Cross, European Region, Berlin, Germany

Coordinate communications for greater Germany area. Work with 16 service groups to develop written standards for Red Cross Shelters. Media spokesperson for local and major disasters. Currently writing and designing Web page.

➤ Write newsletters, annual reports, public relations articles, speeches, and fact sheets distributed across Germany and outlying areas, with plans to implement Internet distribution. ← Several mentions of electronic technology important because international communications demands Internet & online publishing competency.

➤ Initiate and plan media relations, publicity events, annual meetings, and projects (designers/printers) for Red Cross endeavors; working with team of 11.

1994-1995   **Public Relations Assistant**, International Publicité, Paris, France

Designed and produced copy for 12 brochures, 12 proposals, and 5 presentations in France. Developed Web page and company Internet-published magazine. Led team of 17 developing PR proposals. Coordinated mailings. Maintained employee morale during rumors of pending bankruptcy. "Ms. Quito was indispensable. We would have lost half our employees if she had not remained calm, continuing to produce for our clients," according to Jacque DuPris, Senior Public Relations Manager. ← Includes praise from a supervisor.

1993-1994   **Manager**, Law School Records and Admit Specialists, Paris, France

Managed publication, sales, and distribution for $20 million nonprofit legal education services organization. Promoted company's 16 publications

(1 of 2)

Sentence break on first page signals reader there is a second page.

Lorna Quito

through direct marketing, law school forums, and book publishers. Established positive relationship with press, radio, and television contacts. Led creative team of 14 members to develop effective publicity strategies.

1984-1992   Cooper-Cologne, U.S. Division, Los Angeles, CA

(1988-1992) **Senior Coordinator of Publicity Services** for $45 million management consulting company with offices in 18 countries. Managed 8 activities and 41 staff members involved in database development, list purchase, publication schedule, and in-house communications.

(1984-1988) **Special Projects Coordinator:** Planned logistics of monthly executive forums in selected U.S. cities. Directed key facets of annual 200-member business conferences for U.S. and Canadian markets.

Education

1981, Bachelor of Fine Arts, cum laude; The Mary and Joseph Institute, Maryland
1994-1996, Riddell University, Los Angeles; courses in journalism

Place highest education first, although noting more recent education. Modest GPA not mentioned.

When hand delivered, this creative person's resume lends itself to portfolio treatment (showing samples of your work). Because RezReaders say they want less, not more, paper, think about making two collections of portfolio content:

Collection 1: The "pony pack" contains just two or three outstanding examples of public relations coups, such as major feature stories featuring your client.

Collection 2: The "race horse pack" contains a more generous representation of your public relations success. During a job interview, begin with Collection 1, holding Collection 2 in reserve until you receive signals the timing is right to offer more.

Restaurant Manager
REVERSE CHRONOLOGICAL/COMPUTER FRIENDLY

Trisha S. Dunbar
123 Massachusetts Street, Salem, Kansas 66146   (913) 345-9876   E-mail: dunba@aol.com

Objective

General Manager position in a fast-paced, family-oriented restaurant

> Note: The apostrophe after "years" replaces "of."

Summary of Qualifications

- 14 years' experience in family-oriented restaurant management
- Implemented strategic marketing plan which increased patronage 43% at Maggie McGee's
- Designed award system for waitstaff, increasing sales 36% and decreasing employee turnover
- High energy and optimism motivate employees, thereby increasing guest satisfaction
- Graduated summa cum laude with Bachelor's in Business Management while working full-time

Professional Experience

1992-present   **General Manager**   Maggie McGee's, Salem, Kansas
Direct operations of this family-oriented restaurant which serves over 600 meals daily.
Oversee activities of 6 assistant managers, supervising staff of 150.

> Notes specific customer base.

- Developed marketing plan, increasing business by 43%
- Implemented new computer system which decreased degree of error by 25%
- Redesigned kitchen for greater efficiency and ease of movement
- Programmed computer system for new restaurant in Missouri

1988-1992   Assistant Manager   Teller's Restaurant, Lawrence, Kansas
Assisted general manager with guest satisfaction, daily operations, staffing, inventory control,
training, and business and marketing plans. Supervised staff of 100, serving over 400 meals daily.

- Designed and implemented computer program to assist in staffing
- Implemented training program which restaurant chain adopted as company policy
- Assisted general manager in developing marketing plan, increasing business 18%
- Designed program for greater inventory control, decreasing loss 26%

> Gives documentable results.

1983-1986   **Bar Manager**   The Lion's Roar, Chico, California
Responsible for guest satisfaction, staffing, inventory control, policy implementation, budget
control, and marketing and promotional plans. Supervised staff of 25, serving 500 customers
daily.

- Developed promotional plans that increased student business by 55%
- Assisted restaurant managers in developing staff award system
- Developed "Home-We-Go," an alcohol awareness program offering rides to bar guests

1981-1983   **Head Cocktail Server**   The Lion's Roar, Chico, California
Responsible for guest satisfaction, responsible alcohol service, and daily scheduling.

- Improved scheduling system, increasing efficiency and eliminating confusion
- Promoted to Bar Manager

> Including this position and promotion indicates that Dunbar has substantial restaurant experience prior to her management experience.

Education

Bachelor of Arts in Business Management with minor in Computer Science
California State University at Chico, Chico, CA, 1983
Honors: Summa Cum Laude; GPA 3.95/4.0

Real Estate Agent
REVERSE CHRONOLOGICAL/COMPUTER UNFRIENDLY

∘∘∘∘∘∘∘∘∘∘∘∘∘∘∘∘∘∘ **Tanner Childs** ∘∘∘∘∘∘∘∘∘∘∘∘∘∘∘∘∘∘

4190 Parkside, New Rochelle, New York 10801 (212) 720-0504
E-mail: tchilds@cdl.com   Pager: (212) 485-7894

∘∘∘

Note pager and e-mail -- current with technology.

Summary
More than 12 years' real estate and financial experience. Skilled in negotiating and administering subcontractor submittals, architectural draftings, cost containment and recoveries contracts, estimates, bid packages, project development, and field work.

Computer reads hollow bullets as letter "o," thus name becomes "ooTanner Childsoo" and bulleted items become "oProcurement," "oPrimary," and so on.

Experience
1993 - Present   **Franklin Contractors Corporation,** Financial Specialist
New York City, NY
FCC is the Federal Deposit Insurance division for failed savings and loan liquidation.

Briefly describes prestigious employer.

1996-1997   **Contract Specialist -- New Rochelle, NY**
∘ Procurement and administration of 93 financial service and consulting contracts valued at $100 million
∘ Primary Contract Administrator for 12 firms, including Lloyd & Donner, Hilteron Consulting, and Carrington & Associates
∘ Contract oversight on 32 payroll contracts with Hill Services, valued at more than $17 million
∘ Advisor to U.S. Office of Inspector General and Office of Contractor Oversight and surveillance for contractor billing acquisitions of failed thrifts; conducted over 100 training seminars for agents

Names prestigious clients in field.

1993-1995   **Operations /Loan Portfolio Consultant -- New Rochelle, NY**
∘ Advisor to acquiring bank executive management on operational mergers and acquisitions of failed thrifts, conducted training seminars for agents. Redding Banks, Green Banks, NY Financial.

Consulting background verified by naming clients.

1985-1993   **Wholesale Loans Inc. Vice President -- New Rochelle, NY**
∘ Managed sales department -- $4 billion in loan volume
∘ Originated wholesale of 37 mortgage loan packages

Education
Bachelor of Science, Business Economics, University of California, Santa Barbara, 1981

Professional Licenses and Designations
New York: General Contractor's License, Real Estate Brokers License, Notary Public
California Real Estate License
Residential Member, American Institute of Real Estate Appraisers
Warranted Contract Officer, Resolved Trust Corporation
Member, National Contracting Management Association

Sales Representative
REVERSE CHRONOLOGICAL/COMPUTER UNFRIENDLY

 R.S.

Richard Stanton

321 Ranch Lake Road, Houston, Texas 77081   (713)664-5678

> Stanton seeks to widen net for jobs, hence term "technical" frequently substituted for "auto."

Objective

Sales Representative position with technical and marketing focus. 20 years' sales, training, marketing, operations, and management experience in automotive industry.

Work History

President, Conversion Products, Inc., 1996-Present

◆ Relocated and streamlined manufacturing plant, recertified testing lab according to EPA
◆ Increased sales 28% in first quarter of 1996

President, Motoran Corporation, 1988-1996

◆ Increased sales 84% in eight years by revising product line, opening new distribution channels, and expanding markets
◆ Engineered new product development, supervising team of 45 sales representatives
◆ Provided technical service and support to resolve client dissatisfaction

Director, Auto-Serve Center, 1985-1988

> "Director" substituted for "Owner" of business to seem more [illegible] taking direction.

◆ Invigorated repair shop by strengthening team work, productivity, and cost control
◆ Initiated a 527% sales increase and achieved first-year profit goals in three months
◆ Led national sales in October 1997 out of 100 Auto-Serve Centers

Technical Service Manager, Good Tire Corporation, 1982-1985

◆ Managed product engineering, quality assurance, warranty administration, and technical marketing activities for replacement parts division
◆ Supervised 37 chief and staff engineer activities
◆ Integrated technical activities into domestic and international sales and distribution, including trade show participation and international travel

Service Training Manager, Truckline Inc., 1981-1983

◆ Led customer technical service and training; instructed 112 staff
◆ Involved in ad agency operations and coordination of 9 trade shows
◆ Established team of 90 national distributors in two years

Education

Master of Business Administration, University of Texas at Austin, Austin, TX, 1994
Bachelor of Science, Industrial Technology, Southern University, Dallas, TX, 1980

> Omitted lengthy list of automotive publications and professional affiliations to avoid typecasting.

> Computer will gag on graphics and decorative typeface at top.

Editor
TARGETED/COMPUTER UNFRIENDLY

Ron Bohart-Smithy

123 Albany Road, College Park, MD 20742
(301) 456-7891   E-mail: 1111,222@compuserve.com

> Resume could be made computer friendly by moving e-mail address to separate line below the telephone number. Computer will read numerical e-mail address as a street address.

Position as Sunbright Community Newspapers publisher and business manager, using more than 15 years' experience in print media publishing and management.

Summary of Qualifications

- Unassailable record of increasing sales and cost-containment management of newspapers, magazines, shoppers and journals. Experienced in supervising temporary workforce.

- Launched shopper: current circulation 50,500, grew revenues in 18 months to $40,000 per issue.

- Dynamo in business area -- increased profits to highest point in four years for leading industry guide. Trimmed costs by 18%.

Summary of Skills

- PUBLISHING SKILLS: In-depth knowledge of weekly and free-circulation newspaper industry -- Awarded by National Newspaper Association for outstanding weekly.
- RAINMAKING SKILLS -- Boosted ad revenues for 100,000 weekly circulation by 300% in one year; enjoy civic activities with community leaders.
- MANAGEMENT SKILLS -- Produced largest issues in recent history for 85,000-circulation weekly.

Accomplishments and Experience

> Note larger font size used to hook reader, smaller size for job description fill-in.

- **Successfully started a new business newspaper**
Reader's Business Journal, Baltimore, MD   September 1995-February 1997

  As General Manager, launched gazelle business journal for Pale Moon Printing, opening its office and hiring, supervising and training all staff.
  - Publication currently maintains free-circulation exceeding 50,500.
  - Grew revenues from 0 to $40,000 per issue.

> Note high-impact presentation of achievements & experience.

- **Increased profits to highest point in four years, established leading industry guide**
Georgetown Associates, Washington, DC   June 1994-May 1995

  As Publisher, directed newspapers, magazines and books for coin and paper money collectors at world's largest hobby publisher. Trained new editors newsstand techniques to increase sell-through.

  Georgetown News, Minter's Economy Reporter, and Penny Prices.
  - Total distribution exceeded 200,000. Sold a new $200,000 per year ad insert contract.

(1 of 2)

Ron Bohart-Smithy

- **Won award for finest large weekly (managed three with 30 employees)**
PDR Publishing, Northampton, MA and Boston, MA   November 1991-May 1994

    As Group Manager and Publisher, superintended three weeklies with 85,000 circulation.
    - Direction of 30 full-time employees led to surpassing sales goals.
    - Won Boston Press "Sweepstakes" for finest large weekly, listed in 1993 "Who's Who."

- **Quadrupled advertising sales at the National Newspaper Association**
Publisher's Auxiliary, NNA, Boston, MA   December 1987-November 1991

    As General Manager, supervised trade publication, recognized as the leading "how to" guide in the field.
    - Personally cited as NNA's most valuable service in member survey.
    - Judged National Best Paper Contest.
    - Represented NNA at state press meetings, Amer-Eastern Shows and American Press, familiarizing and selling with newspaper executives and vendors.

- **Launched new, special sections in subsidiary of Worrell, managed employees**
Daily Voice, Worrell Newspapers, Albany, NY   October 1985-December 1987

    As Co-operative Advertising Manager, oversaw circulation of 31,000 daily, solicited manufacturers and distributors, launched successful new sections.

- **Produced largest issues in the recent history for an 85,000 free-circulation weekly**
"10-Storey" (news & Hebrew weekly), Albany, NY   April 1984-September 1985

    As Publisher, produced three weeklies and supervised 45 employees.

- **Promoted publication to nation's finest small weekly, 11 awards, record profits.**
New England Talk, Bangor, ME   February 1983-March 1984

    As Publisher, increased paid circulation to an all-time high of 14,083, increasing ad lineage; New England Talk showed record profits.
    - Awarded by National Newspaper Association as nation's finest small weekly.
    - 11 awards from the Maine Press Association.

Education
Bachelor of Arts, Marketing, University of Boston, MA
Dean's List in Major, awarded for outstanding performance.

Nonprofit Manager
REVERSE CHRONOLOGICAL/COMPUTER FRIENDLY

MARSHA ANN WHITELAND

231 Montrose Heights   (603) 456-9876
Manchester, NH 03104   E-Mail: mwhite@mci.mail.com

....

NONPROFIT MANAGER-ATTORNEY: Significant experience with urban issues and nonprofit organizations. Successful manager of complex multimillion-dollar programs requiring constant attention to bottom line. Skilled advocate effective in stressful environment requiring personal diplomacy mediation among conflicting groups.

....

Nonprofits struggle for funds; a manager who is an attorney is a value-added candidate -- a resume opener.

PROFESSIONAL EXPERIENCE

STANFORD RESOLUTION, INC., Montpelier, Vermont

Senior Counsel, Professional Liability Section, June 1997 to present

Manage professional liability (34 members including section chiefs, attorneys, paralegals, and clerical staff), and substantive legal work involving approximately 175 failed savings and loans. Close investigations, bring suit, and settle litigation. "With Marsha in charge, we are a legal powerhouse!" -- Jack Ricemaster, Co-Senior Counsel.

Quantifies all achievements.

Upward mobility shown by dividing jobs by heading.

Counsel, Professional Liability Section, November 1991 to May 1997

Quantifies all achievements.

Managed investigation and litigation of civil claims against 25+ failed savings and loans, as well as liaisoned with attorneys, accountants, brokers, appraisers, insurers, and fidelity bond companies; supervised investigators and counsel, assuring cost-effectiveness. Budgeted more than $15 million for S&L project. Coordinated with federal agencies: Department of Justice, Office of Thrift Supervision, and Federal Deposit Insurance Corporation.

Shows results with achievements.

OSWALD, LEICHT, AND SCHULTZ, Washington, D.C.
Associate, September 1989 to September 1991

Focused civil litigation on real estate issues, HUD regulations, and franchise laws.

Minimizes less pertinent jobs.

LEAGUE OF FEMALE CITIZENS' FUND, Washington, D.C.
Project Director, October 1985 to September 1989

Includes apt volunteer services in work history.

Directed 100+ volunteers in national Community Development Block Grant Monitoring Project; executed volunteer training program; organized national conference allowing volunteer participant conferences with officials of Department of Justice and Housing and Urban Development .

Shows results with achievements.

EDUCATION

STANFORD LAW SCHOOL, Juris Doctorate, Bar Admission, Washington, D.C.

NEW HAMPSHIRE UNIVERSITY, Bachelor of Arts, Urban Studies, Magna Cum Laude

Freelance Graphic Artist

HYBRID & TARGETED/COMPUTER UNFRIENDLY

> Computer sees e-mail address too close to telephone number.

MICHELLE M. SMARTS
123 National Ave., Apt. B, Wise, VA 24293

Graphic designer/5 yrs exp/Virginia
(703) 456-7891, E-mail: arts@iii.com

OBJECTIVE: Graphic designer for medical center.

HIGHLIGHTS OF EXPERIENCE:

> Advanced degrees count in targeting academic setting of medical center.

Education: Master of Arts, Graphic Design, 1996
Graduate Program, University of Virginia at Richmond,
Division of Biomedical Visualization

Graphic Designer and Artist Programmer
See Biomedical Visualization departmental WWW home page, University of Virginia,
Richmond

> Clean layout emphasizes design skills as well as mastery of computer skills.

Broad-based experience in computer and hard copy image processing skills:

computer animation	3-D modeling	Web page graphics
graphic design	interactive multimedia	production graphics
HTML programming	Internet home page	book layout

> Maximizes white space by using columns. Stand-alone words are OK in columns, but not in text. Vertical lines are not computer friendly.

Software skills:

Macromedia Director	Adobe Illustrator	Imageworks XV	NetScape
Visual Basic	Freehand	PageMaker	Mosaic
HyperCard	Photoshop	QuarkXPress	MacromediaPro
CorelDRAW!	Photostyler	PowerPoint	Infini-D
	Lumena	Persuasion	Crystal 3-D
		Alias	

> Includes KeyWords in all skills listings.

Freehand imaging skills:

high rendering	photography	pastel/pencil	oil painting
life drawing	airbrush	pen & ink	biological imaging
sculpting	charcoal	watercolor	

> Showcases most pertinent experience on first page.

EMPLOYMENT:

Freelance Illustrator, Lexington, Virginia   1996-Present

> Illustration of medical poster, advertisement and manual images, computer graphics, logos, NetScape and Mosaic home page design. Captain and collaborate with a team of seven artists.

Graphic Design Intern, Presbyterian Hospital, Wise, Virginia   1995-Present

> Illustration and graphic design for health and medical-related subjects. Primary focus on creative advertising of medical services and health care plans. Campaign resulted in $225K revenue increase.

(1 of 2)

MICHELLE M. SMARTS

Graduate Assistant, Computing Systems Aid, University of Virginia   1993-1994

    Updating and troubleshooting existing computer systems, instructing 375 of students, alumni and faculty in use of all software on Macintosh and DOS/Windows systems.

Illustrator and Computer Consultant, Word Crafts, Butterfield, Virginia   1992-1993

    Page layout and illustration for products and product labels, graphic design for advertisements and catalogues, new product design and development, updated production system and streamlined and computerized all corporation's file storage.

ASSOCIATIONS AND HONORS:

Association of Medical Illustrators, 1995-Present
International Interactive Communications, 1996-Present
Graduate Student Council, Communications Chair, 1995-1996
Distinguished Student, 1992-1994

COMPLIMENTARY QUOTES:

> Maximizes 2nd page with humanizing testimonials.

"It's important to be able to distinguish between a good designer and a great designer; Michelle distinguishes herself!"
-- Dr. Mary Landsforth, Director of Presbyterian Hospital Communications Department

"I thought *I* was the hot computer imaging genius, until Smarts came along and taught *me!*"
-- Kyle Day, Resident Programmer, Div. of Biomedical Visualization, University of Virginia

"When Michelle joined us, we all had to work a little harder -- her speed and originality made us look bad by comparison!"
-- Lizel Delosrios, Lexington computer graphics freelancer

> Newer scanner software can read italics; old ones can't. Smarts called her target medical center and determined they have newer software. When in doubt, don't use italics.

Speech-Language Pathologist
PROFESSIONAL & TARGETED/COMPUTER FRIENDLY

Brian N. Hawes
123 Northumbridge Avenue Nashville, Tennessee 37203
(615) 456-7891   E-mail bhaw@aol.com

> Replaces objective with job title.

→ **Speech-Language Pathologist**

EDUCATION

1989 to 1991, and 1998   **University of Tennessee, Chattanooga, TN**
Ph.D., 1991; dissertation pending.
Minor: Audio/Visual Media, G.P.A: 4.00   > Includes top achievements.
Awarded assistantship for clinical research.
1987 to 1988   **Wolgrel University, Bartlett, TN**
Master of Science in Speech-Language Pathology, Minor: Psychology, G.P.A.: 4.00
Wrote and produced radio and television commercials and promotional videos.
1978 to 1982 and 1988   **Tuskeegee University, Tuskeegee, TN**
Bachelor of Arts in Language, Minor: History, G.P.A.: 3.86
Graduated summa cum laude, after three study-abroad terms, serving as multimedia laboratory
assistant, student government representative, and club president.

> Skips summary-- saved for cover letter.

> Shows extra-curricular achievements.

PROFESSIONAL EXPERIENCE AND ACCOMPLISHMENTS

1990 to Present   **Radius Vox Laboratories, Millington, TN**   **Director**
Firm delivers computer and video imaging and audio signal analysis (voice spectrography). Marketing
targets hundreds of physicians and healthcare providers treating laryngeal, craniofacial dental, and
neurologic disorders.

> Describing prestigious employer.

1989 to 1990   **University of Tennessee, Chattanooga, TN**   **Lecturer, Researcher**
Restructured research laboratory, adding new facilities for voice analysis, videoendoscopy, and
biofeedback. Employed sound spectrography, stroboscopy, photography, and electrophysiologic
measurement techniques. Lectured to 233 Linguists on articulation and voice disorders analysis.
Supervised Orofacial Clinic (staff of 37), developed familiarity with fiberoptic endoscopy,
videofluoroscopy, and nasometry.

> Quantifies achievements.

1988 to 1990   **The Sound & Sight Center, Bartlett, TN**   **Speech-Language Pathologist**
Provided assessment and therapy to over 3,000 patients (neurologic, orofacial, vocal and pediatric).
Designed medical forms and computer based therapy, decreasing procedure time by 30%. Coordinated
patient referral plans with local medical centers.

> Shows industry knowledge.

OTHER SKILLS AND CERTIFICATIONS
Computer: Windows (latest version), numerous applications, Microsoft certified, AI (Prolog), SAS, and SPSS.
Specialized Certifications: American Speech Association, International Association of Forensic Phonetics,
Association of Phonetic Sciences, Zertifikat Deutsch, Goethe Institute Summer Abroad Fellowship, and Lake
Search and Rescue Team. Licensed Tennessee Speech-Language Pathologist, FCC Radiotelephone Operator's
Permit.

Financial Executive

LINEAR/COMPUTER FRIENDLY

Contact information placed on right so it can be read easily when RezReader thumbs through a stack of resumes.

Diana Carter
12 Wollenstromcraft Way
Princeton, NJ 07921
(908) 345-6789
dcart@aol.com

Objective: FINANCIAL MARKETS MANAGEMENT POSITION

Experience:

Great Eastern Bank, Princeton, NJ   July 1993-July 1998
Second Vice President -- Global Markets Project Manager
• Developed, outlined, and scheduled 98 conferences covering spectrum of financial risk
  management issues
• Launched 53-page quarterly newsletter on new products and fluctuations.
  Researched and edited copy from technical specialists and regulatory agencies
• Expanded circulation of client newsletter more than 500% in three years
• Managed $1.2 million budget and monitored department expenses
• Provided marketing support for Senior Vice President
• Traveled to Hong Kong, Singapore, and London delivering educational seminars on
  derivative products and uses
• Administered 17 bank personnel policies for seven staff members
• Directed office closure due to downsizing

Divides job by title, emphasizing upward mobility.

Reason for leaving OK here -- widespread banking mergers.

Assistant Treasurer -- Global Risk Managment Project Coordinator
• Assisted establishment of Risk Management Education & Marketing department
• Created presentation materials for over 30 conferences and education programs in 1994
• Promoted to Project Manager/Second Vice President

PC Leaser Inc., Newark, NJ   November 1990-June 1993
Assistant Vice President
• Negotiated and prepared loan documentation for 23 financing lease transactions
• Scheduled and finalized fundings with 15 financial institutions

Trims down less relevant jobs to focus resume on target job.

Computer Borrowers Corporation, New York City, NY   May 1989-November 1990
Lease Finance Administrator
• Managed company's secured credit lines, market activity, and interest rates
• Arranged financing for transactions up to $2 million and interim financing for all leases
• Served as financial liaison with 5 departments within the company

Education:

Graduate School of Management, University of New York, New York City
• Currently pursuing an MBA (part-time), credits earned: 38 of 60
Cambridge College, Cambridge, MA
• Bachelor of Arts in Sociology, May 1986

GPA not high, thus not mentioned.

Part V
The Part of Tens

The 5th Wave   By Rich Tennant

"Ooh—I think we've found our man."

In this part ...

Good things happen in tens — at least, in this part they do. Here you'll find things to do and not to do, tips for finding a professional resume writer (not that you'll need one), and a checklist that you can use to score your own KickButt resume. Have at 'em.

Chapter 15

Ten (× 3) Ways to Prove Your Brags

. . . .

. . . .

*T*he easy part of resume creation is reading about it in books like this. Now comes the tough part: inventing accomplishments. You'll have to summon up your best creative talents to design workplace successes that are impossible to check. Of course, I'm kidding. But that's what a RezReader will think you've done if your resume alleges wondrous deeds without the support of verifiable evidence.

Highly creative in home arts area; excellent communications skills, more than a decade of experience in writing and publishing; nationally recognized as lecturer and consultant…

And? So? Why should anyone care? What's wrong with this word picture? Answer: The tribute is nice enough, but the description neglects a key KickButt factor — *measurable good results!*

The KickButt factor kicks in when you add credibility with certifiable, tangible information.

Quantify your accomplishments when you want to persuade.

For example, suppose a television commercial asserts that Brand X cola is a better drink than Brand Y cola. What a yawn. But when the commercial switches to report a study in which 70 percent of those tested prefer Brand X cola, the boast sounds plausible. Another quick example: Aren't you more impressed by commercials that say, "Nine out of 10 doctors recommend Blue Company aspirin," than those that merely claim, "Blue Company aspirin is the best"?

The message for KickButt RezWriters is quantify, quantify, quantify! Use these three main quantitative methods to boost the plausibility of your accomplishments: *numbers, percentages,* and *dollar amounts.*

Quantifying the example at the beginning of this chapter, the word picture now moves into the KickButt class of self-marketing materials. Here's how someone like homestylist Martha Stewart might do it:

> *Created* Martha Stewart Living, *a home arts magazine with $50 million annual ad revenues; featured in Martha Stewart Living, a syndicated television program distributed by Group W Productions to 140 stations; author of 12 best-selling home arts books, published since 1982 by Crown Publishing/ Random House; give 12 lectures per year, $15,000 honorarium for each; consultant to Kmart stores, completed $1 million-a-year consulting contract, still receive royalties for sheets, towels, and paint creations.*

I repeat: quantify, quantify, quantify. Look at the following statements in the three categories of numbers, percentages, and dollar amounts. Fill in the appropriate blanks. You're doing this as an exercise to remind you to quantify your accomplishments and results — anything you're proud of. This numbers game works in virtually any occupation or industry.

Supporting your high performance with numbers, percentages, or dollar amounts takes the sting out of bragging. Regardless of your line of work — a trainer counting 5,000 people instructed, a molecular biology manager sequencing 10 dsRNA genes of reovirus serotype 3, or a fast-food manager noting $3,000 in janitorial supplies saved — don't forget to make your numbers!

Say It with Numbers

1. _____ (#) years of extensive experience in _____

   and _____ .

2. Won _____ (#) awards for _____

   _____ .

3. Trained/Supervised _____ (#) full-time and _____ (#) part-time employees.

4. Recommended by _____

   _____ (a number of notable people)

   as a _____ (something good that they said about

   you) for excellent _____ (an accomplishment or skill).

5. Supervised a staff of _____ (#).

6. Recruited _____ (#) staff members in _____ (period of time,)

   increasing overall production.

7. Sold _____ (# of products) in _____ (period of time), ranking _____

   (1st, 2nd, 3rd) in sales in a company of _____ (#) employees.

8. Exceeded goals in _____ (#) years/months/days, establishing my employer

   as _____ (number — 1st, 2nd, 3rd) in industry.

9. Missed only _____ (#) days of work out of _____ (#) total.

10. Assisted _____ (#) (executives, supervisors, technical directors, others).

Say It with Percentages

1. Excellent _____ (your top proficiency) skills, which resulted in _____ (%) increase/decrease in _____ (sales, revenues, profits, clients, expenses, costs, charges).

2. Recognized as a leader in company, using strong skills to effect a/an _____ (%) increase in team/co-worker production.

3. Streamlined _____ (industry procedure), decreasing hours spent on task by _____ (%).

4. Used extensive _____ (several skills) to increase customer/member base by _____ (%).

5. Financed _____ (%) of tuition/education/own business.

6. Graduated within the top _____ (%) of class.

7. Responsible for an estimated _____ (%) of employer's success in _____ (functional area/market).

8. Resolved customer relations issues, increasing customer satisfaction by _____ (%).

9. Eliminated _____ (an industry problem), increasing productivity by _____ (%).

10. Upgraded _____ (an industry tool), resulting in _____ (%) increase in effectiveness.

Say It with Dollar Amounts

1. Supervised entire _____ (a department) staff, decreasing middle management costs by _____ ($).

2. Purchased computer upgrade for office, saving the company _____ ($) in paid hours.

3. Eliminated the need for _____ (one or several positions in company), decreasing payroll by _____ ($).

4. Averaged _____ ($) in sales per month.

5. Collected _____ ($) in memberships and donations.

6. Supervised the opening/construction of new location, completing task at _____ ($) under projected budget.

7. Designed entire _____ _____ program, which earned _____ ($) in company revenues.

8. Implemented new _____ system, saving _____ ($) daily/weekly/monthly/annually.

9. Reduced cost of _____ (substantial service) by developing and implementing a new _____ system at the bargain price of _____ ($).

10. Restructured _____ (organization/system/product) to result in a savings of _____ ($).

Chapter 16
Ten Resume Myths Exposed

*L*ong-cherished notions deserve a second look in today's uncertain times. Here's a brief examination of some popular myths.

The Only-One-Right-Way Myth

Perhaps you've read "inside wire" advice in which an expert insists that two ways exist to prepare resumes — the expert's way and the wrong way. Unfortunately, the experts don't agree. You'd think that after a half a century of wrestling with the issues, by now everyone would be painting on the same canvas. Not so — the debates continue with theological intensity.

Squabbles concern topics such as these: Which length is best — one page, two pages, more? Which format is best — reverse chronological or functional format? Which opening is best — objective or summary?

When I began writing about careers, I was puzzled by the great resume debates. Why were people landing interviews and jobs, despite their breaking various so-called rules of resume writing? Why was I seeing great resumes crash and burn, and trash resumes producing interviews and jobs? Finally, the dawn broke. *There is no one best way.* There are no absolutes in resume writing. There is only the best judgment of advisers, including myself. The reason career experts differ is because the human experience differs. For resumes, the old cliché is true: different strokes for different folks.

The best resume for you is the one that best supports your quest for a job interview. I offer suggestions and guidelines, but have you ever noticed how solutions to problems always seem to work better in books? The message: You may have to experiment a bit before you graduate into the KickButt crowd.

The Myth of the 90-Minute Resume

Saying that a KickButt resume can be written in 90 minutes or overnight is like saying Michelangelo could have made better time with a roller. Good work takes effort.

The No-Fun-at-All Myth

You need not always use a straight pitch, nor confine your creative input to a choice between white and ivory stationery. But when you feel compelled to come up with clever ways to catch an employer's eye, be dead sure you know your audience and how the resume will be received by the RezReader. If you apply to a traditional, conservative field such as banking or accounting, stick to the tried and true. Otherwise your resume will be seen as frivolous and unbusinesslike, attracting the kind of attention a curio draws, but not leading to an interview.

Having given you fair warning, I believe there certainly are times when you should take a chance. If you decide to field a quirky resume that shows you put thought into it and didn't just grind it out, deliver it into the hands of hiring managers — not human resource department specialists. That's because HR specialists are paid to screen out risky applicants; if you submit fluff stuff, you're risky. Hiring managers, who make selections from a pre-screened candidate pool, may be intrigued enough to see you.

The One-Page-or-Bust Myth

The fallacy that a resume must be kept to one page should be titled *Resume with a Vampire*. It just won't die and stay dead. Drive a stake through its heart.

The reality is: Your resume should be as long as needed to get your concise message across with zip and punch.

Human resource specialists recommend one pagers because they save reading time.

Recognize that you and human resource specialists do not share the same goal. Their goal is to effectively screen applicants as quickly as possible. Your goal is to present your qualifications as strongly as possible.

Resume superstar Richard H. Beatty is another person who thinks that doctrinaire demands for one-page resumes shortchange job seekers. Beatty is president of Brandywine Consulting Group in Westchester, Pennsylvania, a corporate outplacement consulting firm. He says that after 30 years as a corporate employment professional, he believes that forcing individuals who have ten or more years of experience to shoehorn it into a single page will cause the "omission of major accomplishments and significant contributions." Beatty says, in such cases, a format of two pages is better.

Electronic resumes raise other issues about length. Because your resume remains in databases for long periods of time, you will be considered for more than one job. Suppose you, a registered nurse, submitted a resume to a health facility for a specific job but missed out. Six months later a department manager may telephone the facility's human resources manager: "Sally, can you run a search for an oncology nurse?" If the word "oncology" is on your resume, you'll be considered for the job; if not, you won't. The more information you give, the greater the chances of an electronic hit. While you can accomplish this with an opening summary of keywords, somewhere in your resume each KeyWord must be supported by a citation.

My advice: One page for new graduates, one to two pages for most people, and two to three pages for senior executives.

The Fibs-Are-Fine Myth

Blowing smoke on your resume — inflating grades, inventing degrees, concocting job titles — is assumed to be risk free because nobody checks, and because the resume is not a legal document. Wrong. Once you lie, you have no easy way out. People do check, especially in competitive times when a RezReader's job may be on the line for not checking. Trained interviewers are taught to ask you the same question several ways, spotting inconsistencies. Even if you fib your way into a job, your little lie is a time bomb in your personnel file — tick, tick, tick.

The Typewriter-Will-Do Myth

The difference between computer printouts and typewriter stomping is obvious: the latter leaves the paper lumped with key impressions. In joining the computer crowd, you show yourself to be up-to-date and able to handle office demands for word processing, a serious concern for job seekers over 40.

The ultimate reason why your computer resume is a stand-out and your typewriter resume a throw-out is the finished product: You can make it flawless in a flash, without running to the office supply store to buy a bottle of white-out.

The Resume-Does-It-All Myth

Your resume is only one marketing tool in your job search that can help you get an interview. Once you get the interview, it all depends on you. *You* are what gets you a job — your skills, your savvy, your personality, your attitude.

Blame Resume for Your Joblessness?

Maybe yes, maybe no. When your resume results in a telephone call from a recruiter, who doesn't issue a come-in-and-see-us invitation, suspect your experience or education. The no-interest response may be an intangible factor discovered in the telephone chat, causing the recruiter to think you're not a good match for the job. Or maybe your resume presents you as a KickButt star, but your telephone manner doesn't deliver the goods.

If your resume results in interviews, but no offers appear on the horizon, maybe you've oversold yourself in a resume, or maybe you just don't know how to close the offer. Brush up on your interviewing skills. *Job Interviews For Dummies* can help.

Can One Resume Do Double-Duty?

Ever more companies use computers to process applicants (see Chapter 1). That's why I recommend either a single KeyWord resume or two resumes — one loaded with action verbs and embellished with bells and whistles for human eyes; the other heavy with nouns and graphically stripped for computers to cuddle. A recent survey of companies suggests recruiters prefer just one version, but the topic is too new for definitive answers. My instinct is to use a KeyWord resume for computers and prepare a second, graphically adorned, verb-rich resume to use when you hand deliver it to the recipient.

The Always-Expect-an-Answer Myth

Job seekers don't understand why employers fail to acknowledge receiving their resumes. *Rude, poor manners, thoughtless — why don't they at least say they received what I sent?* The best companies with plenty of staff and budget do acknowledge resumes. Companies that use job computers to scan resumes into a database have an automatic feature that permits acknowledgment letters to be sent with the click of a key. Small companies with few staff members to review resumes may take a while to respond or may never get around to it if you're not the one. Instead of seething away wondering which tar pit your resume got stuck in, telephone and ask if it was received.

Chapter 17

Ten (× 3) Great Resume Tips

. . . .

. . . .

A KickButt resume carries you upward and onward because it's faster, smoother, brighter, more focused — like you. Here are hard-hitting points to show what you've got.

Tips for Everyone

✔ **Specifically discuss *teamwork* in job descriptions, with examples and results.** RezReaders love this word. They like *team building,* too. Talk about participating in *tough tasks that help focus teams.* Speak of *trust as being essential to teamwork.* Say that you were *part of a team that succeeded in reaching a unified goal.* The difficulty comes in making clear for which portion of the team's production you can take a bow. You must separate your contribution from the group's. If you don't, you chance being looked upon as one who falsely claims credit for work you did not do. If you find room for hobbies, stick to teamplayer sports — volleyball, softball, touch football.

✔ **Unless you're headed for a support job where leadership is a liability, give examples of leadership.** Even as organizational structures flatten by the sunlight hour, every team needs a leader. In the same vein, vision and drive are desirable characteristics. What did you originate, initiate, spearhead, or propose? What have co-workers praised about you? What suggestions have employers accepted from you?

✔ **Discuss an upward track record:** Without giving price tags, style yourself as a winner by mentioning that you received raises, promotions, and bonuses.

✔ **Answer the So What question,** hidden and lying in ambush in every RezReader's mind. Forget sticking to the old name-your-previous-responsibilities routine. Every single time you mention a duty or achievement, pretend someone fires back: *So what, who cares, what does it all mean?* Imagining these questions is not pretending — these are RezReader responses.

Don't just relay what you did — spell out the consequences and implications. A medical technologist might say

- *Organize daily work distribution for effective teamwork of 12 lab workers; absorb and solve workload issues from previous shift.*

- *Monitor quality control; identify problems, find solutions; lab insurance rates, related to mistakes, lowered this year by 3 percent.*

- *Perform preventive maintenance on 14 machines on daily basis; reduced repair costs 8 percent over previous year.*

✔ **Showcase anything that you did in the top 5 percent of company performance ratings.** RezReaders are impressed with the cream of the crop.

✔ **Don't apologize on your resume for any weakness that you may observe in your professional self.** Until you can do something about it, like get additional education or experience, don't even think about shortcomings, and they certainly don't belong on your resume. You're an official KickButter, remember?

✔ **Show how and whom you trained.** RezReaders appreciate the knowledge base suggested by the ability to teach. A smaller company in particular may be run by an entrepreneur whose nightmare is being forced to take time away from running the company to hire and train new people.

✔ **Study the resumes of people in your field.** Seeing how others have handled similar issues is a championship tee-up for writing your own treatment. Libraries have books of resumes for specific career fields. Or look at the thousands of resumes on the Internet. Where to find them? I mention a number of Internet resources in Chapter 1.

✔ **If your career history looks like the fall of the Roman Empire, don't try to explain a lifetime of disasters on a resume.** Save your explanations for an interview. Use your friends and acquaintances to help you obtain interviews. Make the resume as brief and as adversity-free as you legitimately can. At the interview, be prepared to justify your moves, without becoming defensive, and be sure to provide good references.

✔ **Ask a business-savvy friend to read your resume before you send it out.** Prepare a list of questions regarding the comprehensiveness of your resume's explanations and job victories for your friend to answer. It's better to know sooner than later if you're rowing with one oar.

Tips for New Graduates

✔ **The number one tip for new graduates: Attend resume workshops offered at your campus career center or vocational-technical school placement office.** For help in every step of resume development, from drafting to proofing, nothing beats a classroom setting.

✔ **Counselors at your school's career service center can help you understand the prerequisites that individual recruiters look for in their specific career fields.** Target your resume to those prerequisites. *If you cannot qualify for a prerequisite, try to figure out a compensatory benefit you offer.* For example, if your GPA is a little below the prerequisite, use an opening summary to hit hard on knowing the value of hard work — especially if you learned that value by holding a series of demanding student jobs while working your way through school.

✔ Experience, or lack of it, is the biggest obstacle faced by new graduates, especially those who are not employed before they leave school. Employers who don't cruise campuses may be especially reluctant to hire newbies; they fear that new graduates lack the experience to hit the floor running and become immediately productive. Thicken your work experience by including all unpaid positions — internships, special projects, volunteer jobs. List them in chronological order in your *Work Experience* section. Statements like these are powerful agents on your resume:

> • *Sales: Sold $1,200 worth of tickets to college arts festival*
>
> • *Counseling. Advised 16 freshman students, as peer counselor*
>
> • *Public Policy Coordination: Coordinator for student petition drive to save California Cougar from sports hunting, gaining 2,000 signatures in 35 days*

✔ Highlight your work experience that is most relevant to your intended future. If you have more than two years of full-time professional experience, education should be placed at the bottom.

✔ If you use an objective statement, make it clear what objective you have in mind when you get to jobland — don't use a lofty statement of the absurd, like this one:

> • *I'm seeking a challenging position that will allow me to actualize my talents in saving the world, with good potential for professional growth and pay commensurate with my ability.*

✔ Don't just identify your education and a laundry list of student jobs — use words that identify the skills you learned or used in school or at work. "The skill-focused resume wins the [electronic] scanning game!" proclaims a recent issue of the *Journal of Career Planning and Employment,* a publication of the National Association of Colleges and Employers. In a sample resume, the computer found the following list of skills: *clerical, collection, Internet, maintenance, mathematics, property maintenance, quiz, taxation, Windows, Microsoft Word.* A resume-scanning computer can't find what you don't put in your resume. Think of it this way: SIJO — skills in, jobs out.

✔ **Awards, honors, and citations help.** Such items as scholarships, appointments, elections, chairs, and university faculty that holds you in esteem belong in your extracurricular activities or highlights section. Use reverse chronological order.

✔ **Show evidence of dedication and goals;** many RezReaders perceive a lack of commitment and realistic expectations in recent graduates.

✔ **Include your GPA if it is at least 3.0 or high enough for employer prerequisites.** You can limit your GPA to the courses in your major, if necessary, but make it clear that's what you've done. Do not enclose your resume in a report cover or bulky package or attach school transcripts or letters of recommendation, unless they are requested.

✔ **Delete high school data unless it adds a unique fact to the total impression that you're creating.**

✔ **If an activity reveals skills, accomplishments, results, or the qualifications to support your intended job, include it.**

Tips for Seasoned Aces

✔ **Focus your resume.** For emphasis, I'll repeat that: Focus your resume. Concentrate on highlighting your two most recent or relevant jobs. Do not attempt to give equal attention to each of your past jobs. When your job experience has been diversified, your resume may look like popcorn in the making, a job-hopper tale of unrelated job after unrelated job. Focus and concentrate.

✔ **Strive for the aura of youth through concise, crisp writing** that ends before the RezReader's chin hits the desk. Avoid dated words such as *people person, self-starter,* and *go-getter.* Instead: *enjoy interacting with people, self-motivating,* and *motivated to succeed.* This is where you get your chance to show off a mastery of 30 Days to a New Vocabulary.

I have an infallible method to determine whether a term is an age give-away: Find a smart 25-year old and ask, "Do you know what this term means?" If the answer is no, and the term is not a technical term specific to the job you're applying for, replace it.

✔ **Show that you are a tower of strength,** that you recover from downturns with few scars. Give examples of how you solved problems, recovered expenses, and learned to compensate for weaknesses in your working environment. Emphasize how quickly such adjustments occurred. Gray heads who have survived a few fallen skies are valuable assets in difficult times.

✔ **Use buzzwords, KeyWords, and industry terminology** to show your familiarity with important issues in the industry to which you're applying. This tip works across the experience spectrum, but as a seasoned ace, you'll look especially unknowing if you can't talk the talk.

✔ **Demonstrate your political correctness,** especially for positions that have contact with the public. Show that you are familiar with contemporary values by using politically correct terms wherever appropriate. Examples include *multiculturalism, diversity, global community, cross-cultural, mainstream, multiethnic, socioeconomic,* and *people with disabilities* (never *handicapped*). It's an age thing.

✔ **Try shipping your resume over the latest electronic mechanisms** — World Wide Web and e-mail — and you'll help dispel any ideas that you're over the hill. See Chapter 1 for more on electronic resumes.

✔ **Obliterate, annihilate, and liquidate ancient-history dates of your education.** Of course, the absence of dates sends a signal to people who are heavy readers: *This is an old geezer who read a resume book.* But at least it shows that you have sufficient faculties left to play the game. And it beats offering yourself up for sacrifice.

✔ **Assume that your previous job titles will be misunderstood and briefly explain them.** *Marketing manager* may really mean sales, market research, advertising, or all of the above. A regional manager at company A may be a district manager at company B. *Programmer/analyst* is meaningless until the hardware and software are specified.

✔ **Take responsible credit for your previous successes.** Show how you made a difference. Don't go modest on yourself but do go easy on the adjectives. Try to put an appraisal of your worth into someone else's mouth.

✔ **Read through your finished resume in search of anything — from a few words to whole sections — to eliminate or abridge.** For very experienced professionals, sorting out the most powerful resume points can be difficult. It's like being a gifted child — so many choices, and you're good at them all! You know what they say: *The longer the cruise, the older the passengers.*

Special delivery: way-over-the-line gambits

Creative resumes and cover letters are not widely appreciated. But doing something that sets you apart from the great masses of RezWriters can work if you are applying in a creative field, say advertising, marketing, or publicity.

A thoughtful touch may work better to subtly draw attention to yourself. Suppose you research the RezReader and learn of an avid interest in antique cars. If you can find an article on the topic, clip and send it as part of your cover letter, along with your resume. But don't send a book on antique cars — doing so would look like a bribe.

Among the true stories in the following section, the "red shoe man" got the job; the others did not.

On-the-Shoulder Delivery

An in-your-face delivery is what an Ohio job hunter had in mind for his resume. He arrived at the employer's office disguised as a dry-cleaning delivery guy. Slung over his shoulder was a freshly laundered shirt in a see-through plastic bag. Attached to the bag was his resume and a "cover tag" that read: *I'd give the shirt off my back for an interview.*

ABCs of Resumes

A New York advertising agency media buyer smiled when she received a resume and cover letter buried in a box of children's blocks. The blocks spelled: Get Results!

The Red Shoes

A man's red tennis shoe arrived by courier to the Kentucky airline's employment manager. Stuck in the shoe was a resume and a note: *I'd sure like to get my foot in the door.* The ploy worked, and the pilot was interviewed.

Within hours after the interview, a second and much smaller tennis shoe arrived, obviously a child's. This note said: *Thanks for giving my dad the interview!*

High Flyer for Flier

A resume sent to a Kentucky airline human resource manager was attached to a "How to make a paper airplane" kit, trailing a banner that read "*I love to fly.*"

Squeaking Up

An Arizona company received a talking resume. The "press here" button (similar to that found on a talking greeting card), when pressed, caused the imbedded microchip to squeak out the message: *Read me! Read me!* A printed resume was attached.

Nice Try, No Brew

The resume as a miniature beer bottle label is now trite at a Colorado brewery. Ditto the resume as a menu to food companies or a wanted poster to most employers.

References Round-Up

In Illinois, an employment manager was startled to receive a woman's document of references longer than the resume to which it was attached. Each of five pages held three columns of names and addresses — must have been all 72 of her closest friends.

Stay in the Mainstream, Unless . . .

If you have a heavy-duty marketing mind and your approach suits the job you seek, try the resume road less traveled. Otherwise, don't pollute your earnest quest by sending resumes attached to carrier pigeons, or wrapped around a dozen roses, or glued to a chartreuse poster board with a photo of yourself in a bikini. Save your fine imagination for a friend's birthday party.

Chapter 18
Ten (× 3) Common Resume Mistakes

For those who need resume help right this very second, here's a summary of serious resume gaffes to avoid. As in Chapter 17, I've organized the fumbles by groups to which they most apply: anyone, new graduates, and seasoned aces. Although some mistakes occur in one group more than another, it won't hurt you to read every single screwup. It might even help.

Gaffes That Almost Everyone Makes

These are mistakes that anyone can make, regardless of age or experience level.

Excessive vagueness

To keep their options open, many RezWriters mistakenly obscure their intent by stating an objective way too broad, such as "a position in the paper industry." KickButters focus and target, as discussed in Chapter 7. KickButters who offer a summary of qualifications, rather than an objective, define areas of expertise.

Don't expect an employer to dig through your resume to find out whether your qualifications match the job's requirements.

Poor organization

Advice from a California boss: "If it looks complicated, I lose interest." She loses interest in most resumes, she says, because they're tough to comprehend. Double-check your work for construction and focus. Open with either a summary of your qualifications or an objective statement. Headings should be vivid and distinct from one another. Enter each entry under the appropriate heading; that is, put apples with apples, and oranges with oranges — no fruit salad. You don't want to carry the liability of looking disorganized.

One rule of good organization: Find a theme and make certain that every item in your resume supports that theme.

Lack of examples

People who make claims without backing them up with verifiable details are not as credible as those who do back up their claims. Credibility increases with the "storytelling" of solid examples. Rack your reporter's brain for concrete examples of each claim: Ask "Who?" "What?" "When?" "Where?" and "How much?" Weave a convincing tale.

Missing achievements

The missing achievements gaffe is related to the storytelling concept: You must give results. Without results — measured in some way (numbers, percentages, dollar amounts) — that show how you successfully reached high points in your work efforts, your workplace victories will sound as though you made them up.

Irrelevant information

Why tell the RezReader more than the RezReader wants to know? Chapter 5 discusses the obese resume; basically, skip personal information if it doesn't add to the image you're trying to convey. You're selling your professional hours, not your entire life. While you're on litter patrol, delete nontransferable skills and duties and bypass references.

Typos and grammatical oversights

Even the sharpest eyes miss mistakes, so proofread for errors in four steps.

1. **Spell- and grammar-check on the computer.** That's a good start, but don't stop there. Spelling and grammar checkers won't find words that aren't there, ones inadvertently left out. Check the punctuation and grammar: A period often looks like a comma, a *he* like a *she,* and an extra gawky space is often overlooked; a computer won't catch these errors. Furthermore, checkers will approve spellings that represent the wrong word, as this comical but true example, provided by human resource authority Robert Half, illustrates:

   As indicted, I have over five years of analyzing investments.

   Relying totally on machine-driven proofreading reminds me of the gag about the passenger on a completely automated aircraft who asked the plane's voice-activated computer whether the craft was safe. "Don't worry," the computer replied. "Nothing can go wrong. . . nothing can go wrong. . . nothing can go. . ."

2. **Slow down.** Use a ruler to read the entire document aloud, line by line. Speed kills KickButt resumes.

3. **Read backward, from the bottom up.** Start at the lower-right-hand corner, reading backward from the bottom to the top, word by word. You may be a little goofy when you're finished, but, as you are not reading for content, you're likely to spot word warts and other blemishes.

4. **Get a second opinion.** Beg a hawkeyed word mechanic to proof your resume yet one more time. If neither of you can spell a word or find it in a dictionary (I've never understood how you can look up a word you can't spell), change words.

Not checking small details

A number of "little" mistakes cause big rejections. By itself, no single, small flaw is deadly (unless you're applying to be a proofreader). The trouble comes when you add several together on the same resume, collectively zeroing out your chances. A few examples:

- ✔ In a job history, unless you worked for well-known companies, briefly tell the RezReader what the company was in business for. What product does the company make, or what services does it provide?
- ✔ A weak opening produces disinterest.

✔ Using telephone numbers answered by small children or by people who say, "She no longer works here," doesn't help your search.

✔ Highly unusual paper may make you look "too different." Die-cut, oddly shaped, colored paper and fancy binders raise the question of why, if you're such a hot candidate, you need a graphic designer to package you. High-gloss presentations are wasted on electronic resumes — job computers have no taste. Or maybe they do.

An exception to the statement that no one small thing ends your chances is a handwritten update or correction in the margin of your resume. This horrible mistake makes you look lazy and, by itself, is likely to be disqualifying.

Information overload

Many RezWriters forget that *resume* literally means *summary* — to sum up. Their documents suffer from terminal length. Don't let wordiness wreck your resume. Start with a highly selective choice of content and then streamline each item. For example, the statement "Performed managerial functions and delivered employee training" slims down to "Management and training."

Admittedly, it's hard to boil down a lifetime to a page or two or three. Mark Twain said that it took him only five minutes to write a 30-minute speech, but 30 minutes to write a five-minute speech.

Imitating a flat organization

Try to portray yourself as having an upwardly mobile track record even if you've held lateral jobs for years. Mention raises (do not specify amounts) and increasing responsibilities, even if your title never changed. It's human nature for RezReaders to prefer people who seem to be doing better and better over those who are same-o, same-o.

Failing to list all appropriate KeyWords

Because writing electronic resumes is a new bag of tricks to most people, legions of RezWriters do not list every single KeyWord describing their fitness for specific jobs. See Chapter 4 for more information on identifying KeyWords. New ones are created all the time — so pay attention.

Gaffes Common to New Graduates

New graduates and job rookies are more likely to make these mistakes.

Not meeting image standards

Is there no mercy? Just when you finally get the hang of doing term papers, you graduate and, to get on in the world, must learn to do a new kind of paper: your resume. If you present your resume personalized with little printing errors, such as off-centered or crooked placement, ink blotches, or flaws in the paper itself, you flunk. Chapter 9 tells you how to avoid looking like an amateur.

Aiming too high too soon

An imperfect understanding of the world off campus may cause you to indicate in a job objective that the job you're seeking is over your head. You'll be dismissed as naive if you write such aims as becoming "an operations manager in a well-established organization." *Manager* isn't quite the word for an entry-level person, although graduates with several years of experience leading up to a managerial position could swing it. *Well-established organization* may not only exile you from dynamic start-up companies but cause a perception that you expect a lot — perhaps more than an employer can deliver.

Overcompensating with gimmicks

New graduates frequently hear that their resumes are anemic, that they should beef them up. Reversing gears, they may overdo them with too much flash in graphics and language. Don't tart up your resume to cover barren qualifications. Avoid using exotically original language, such as "the eyelinered genius," a term used by a business graduate applying for an entry-level marketing position in the cosmetics industry. The term may be colorful, but charm communicates better in the interview.

Making employers guess

Employers hate it when they are asked to decipher your intent. Merely presenting your declared major and transcript excerpts is not enough to kick off a wowser job search. Either add an objective to your resume or add a skills summary directed at a specific career field. Show potential employers that you've thought about your next move.

Leveling the experience field

Your resume is no place to give every job equal billing. Many rookie resumes are little more than rote listings of previous jobs — subpoena server, TV satellite dish sales representative, waiter, landscape helper, and computer coach, for example. Separate your jobs into an A list and a B list. The A list contains the jobs that relate to what you want to do next, even if you have to stretch them to make a connection. Briefly mention jobs on the B list in a section called *Other Experience* or *Other Jobs*.

Stopping with bare bones

Some new graduates find themselves in a dilemma as irritating as having too much month left at the end of the money. They look at a sheet of paper and then at their embarrassing, bedraggled collection of instant-rice jobs in their paid-experience stew. Desperate to get *anything* on paper, they settle for name, rank, and serial number (employer, job title, and dates of employment).

The solution, says one of my favorite resume authorities, Yana Parker, is to pull in *all* experience, including volunteer and part-time gigs. Sit, think, think some more, and fox out all relevant skills pointing in the direction in which you hope to thumb a ride.

Hiding hot information

Data entombed is data forgotten. RezReaders remember best the information you give first in a resume, not the data smushed in the middle. Decide what your selling points are and pack that punch up front. Ask three friends to read your resume and quickly tell you what they remember about it.

Highlighting the immaterial

Featuring the wrong skills and knowledge attached to each job is an error that many first-time RezWriters make. Suppose you want to be a multimedia producer, and one of your work experience citations is your three years of effort for campus student theatrical productions. You painted scenery, sold tickets, and designed sets. It's the experience in designing sets that helps qualify you for multimedia producer, not painting scenery or selling tickets. Costume yourself in the skills that will help an employer imagine you playing a role in the sought-after work setting.

Ignoring employers' needs

Even the smartest rookies, who may have survived research challenges as rigorous as uncovering the body language of ancient French cave dwellers, make this mistake. They forget to find out what employers want from new hires. In addition to following the standard research techniques mentioned in Chapter 1, if you can find former or present employees willing to share company culture information *from the inside,* go to the head of the KickButt class.

Writing boastfully

Appearing to be too arrogant about your talents can cause RezReaders to question your ability to learn as the junior member on the team. As one recent graduate says, "It's hard to work in a team structure when you're omniscient." Even when you're just trying to compensate for your inexperience, avoid terminology that comes across as contrived or blatantly self-important. If you're not sure, ask older friends to describe the kind of person they think your resume describes.

Gaffes Common to Seasoned Aces

When you've a long job history, you're more likely to need updates on the following issues.

Using old resume standards

Many seasoned aces, still working on last decade's calendar, have an outdated concept of what a resume should be. An ace office neighbor recently expressed surprise when I told him to leave out his personal information, which once was standard fare on resumes. "Oh, I thought personal information was supposed to humanize you," the ace said. Busy RezReaders and job computers don't care that you are a par golfer or play tennis; this kind of personal bonding information comes out at the interview.

Sell performance!

Revealing age negatively

Don't blurt out your age. Your mind-set should be: Start with ageless — you can always move to senior. Do not put old education first on your resume (unless you are a professional educator). Avoid listing jobs with dates older than 10 or 15 years. If you must include dusty jobs, de-emphasize the dates or omit them, as noted in Chapter 10. You can summarize old jobs under a heading of "Prior to 19—" and avoid being too specific. Alternatively, you can include all jobs under functional headings. Try not to describe older jobs in detail.

Words of the past

When you are changing job fields, it's a gigantic error to use jargon from your earlier jobs. Former members of the armed services, in particular, must be alert to militaryspeak that leaves civilian recruiters puzzled. *WESTPAC, O-700,* and *cammies* mean virtually nothing to civilian employers. Write in civilianese. The same warning holds true for anyone who formerly worked in an industry that uses jargon not commonly understood by others. Substitute the jargon with translations or equivalents.

Wrong focus

Choosing the wrong focus is a problem shared with new graduates who have a string of jobs in their background and fail to choose those that best address the hoped-for next job. Try this approach: Use the worksheets in Chapters 7 and 8 to draft an encyclopedic master resume. The number of pages doesn't matter — you'll never use it in its entirety. Each time that you're tailoring a resume for a specific job opening, review your master resume and choose those jobs most directly related to your new goal.

Lack of a summary

Because of the extensiveness of your experience, your resume may be unwieldy without a summary. Usually, it is superfluous to use both an objective and a summary, but exceptions occur. Suppose you're fed up living as a city slicker and want to move to a small town where agribusiness is dominant. Your objective may take only one line — "Wish to work as internal auditor in the farm equipment industry." Follow that statement with a one- or two-paragraph summary of why you are qualified. Think of a summary as a salesperson's hook. It describes some of your special skills, your familiarity with the target industry, and your top achievements. For examples of summaries, see Chapter 8 and the sample resumes in Part IV.

A rule of thumb: If your objective and summary are two ways of saying the same thing, dispense with one of them.

Low-tech appearance

Seasoned aces who do not have computers still type resumes; others with computers have old-fashioned dot matrix printers. Their resumes are often stopped at the door. RezReaders like crisp, attractive layouts that only a computer and laser printer can create. Trade a dinner for resume services from a friend, rent a computer by the hour at a copy center, or pay a professional to do your resume.

Moanin' and groanin'

The stress of job hunting at midlife and older tempts many seasoned aces to reveal professional troubles on their resumes. Big mistake. Unless you, blameless in your terminations, were part of a downsizing, skip reasons why you left. When you explain them in the interview, take the high road and stay positive.

Not considering delivery questions

You've done a real KickButt resume and dropped it in the mail. That may be a shortsighted move.

If you have already contacted a RezReader who is interested and if the job is important to you, consider delivering your resume by hand or by courier service. You can, of course, fax it, but it will lose some of the presentation value you slaved over. Still another alternative is to send it online if you know how to do that and you know that the employer is happy to receive it by e-mail.

When should your resume arrive? Mondays are busy days, and Fridays are termination days; try for arrival on Tuesday, Wednesday, or Thursday.

If you send your resume to a hiring manager, send a duplicate to the human resource department. Note this effort in your cover letter to the hiring manager, which means that not only is the human resource specialist not treated dismissively, but the hiring manager gets to keep your resume as a constant reminder of you instead of having to send it "down to HR."

Not following up

Job seekers who fail to follow up after sending out their resumes stop short of their goals. Always telephone within a few days, making certain that your resume arrived. Ask whether your resume was received and what happened to it. Was your resume scanned into a database? Were you a match for an open position? Was your resume passed on to a hiring manager?

If the answer is "Yes, you're in the database," expect to receive written confirmation within a couple of weeks. (If your resume wasn't received, send another resume and start the cycle over.)

Once your resume is in the database, don't bother calling back the human resource department — you're automatically considered for all open job requisitions. If your resume was passed on to a departmental hiring manager and you can pry loose the manager's name, try calling that manager early in the morning or late in the day.

If the company does not scan resumes into a database, tactics change. Some very smart career advisers suggest calling every ten days until you're told that you'll be arrested if you call again. (You probably won't get the job, either.)

But busy employers insist that, unless you're in a field such as sales and need to demonstrate persistence, call two weeks later and then no more than once every six weeks. Their argument: An excessive number of telephone calls brands you as a nuisance. Instead, try sending interesting short letters or faxes with additional facts about your qualifications, or ideas to solve a problem you know the company is facing, or just to express your continuing interest in working for them.

The time to correct a mistake is before it sends your resume to the isolation ward. The causes of mistakes are: I didn't know it was wrong. . . I didn't think it was important. . . I didn't care enough to find out.

Chapter 19
Ten Resumese Clichés

. . . .

In This Chapter
▶ Troubleshooting for overdone resumese
▶ Substituting fresher alternative language

. . . .

Don't burn your resume if it contains some of these too-familiar phrases — freshen it with newer arrivals. Cliché-free language helps make the KickButt difference.

Hard working. If you are really hard working, you'll work hard for a more believable way to convey this attribute. Begin by highlighting examples of your industriousness, your dedication to the job, and your energetic work ethic. Then add vocabulary such as *motivated, results oriented, driven, goal oriented, achievement oriented, constant follow-through, dedicated, energetic, hard charging, committed,* and *accustomed to a heavy work load.*

Hands-on achiever. This term is a rerun staple. Give examples of your *direct initiative* and of hands-on–type duties that you have performed. If you consider yourself an achiever, try more eye-catching descriptions, such as a summary of accomplishments with quantified results. Or under each job heading, list several achievements. When you demonstrate that you are an achiever, you won't need to say that you're an achiever, and your message will have a more powerful impact.

Bottom-line oriented. Refresh your vocabulary with words that better describe your work ethic, such as *committed to achieving financial goals, budget-driven, focus all efforts on accomplishing financial objectives,* and *pursue budget efficiency.*

Creative innovator. Although this cliché has a nice ring to it, it transmits zippo about you. *Creative* by itself is okay, as long as you accompany it with examples. *Innovator,* however, distresses RezReaders who wish you'd get to the point. Besides being moth-eaten, *creative innovator* is also redundant.

Seeking a challenging opportunity. Who isn't? Not long ago, this phrase was kicker lingo. Not anymore. Try *seeking a demanding position as _____, a rigorous opportunity,* or *the ambitious responsibilities of a_____.*

One of a kind. If you try to call yourself a one-of-a-kind anything, no RezReader — after years of breathing hype instead of fresh air — will believe your fatigued claim. Let your achievements speak for themselves.

Seasoned executive. Almost every executive is a *seasoned executive*. How did you get to be an executive without undergoing seasoning? Instead of sounding dulled by your years of experience, brighten up your image with *steeped in the industry, extensive experience in ___ , extensive track record of ___ , familiar with all aspects of ___ ,* and *long history of positive efforts in ___ .*

Team player. Although you should give examples of teamwork as a concept (see Chapter 17), never label yourself with this frayed-at-the-edges label. RezWriters have so overused the term that no one pays attention to it anymore. Try instead: *collegial, mesh well with coworkers, worked in concert with ___ , collaborated with ___ , team-task minded,* and *achieve shared goals.*

Responsible for . . . This worn-out workhorse is the crutch in a mechanical listing of duties: responsible for this, responsible for that. Ad infinitum. What you should be spotlighting are skills, achievements, and results.

Senior-level executive position. Are there any junior-level executive positions? News to me!

What these resumese clichés can really mean

Some RezReaders have a cynical slant on the most common descriptions. Can you see yourself in any of these?

Exceptionally well qualified: Has not yet blundered into career oblivion

Quick thinking: Offers plausible excuses for mistakes

Takes pride in work: Takes too much pride in self

Forceful and aggressive: Hotheaded and argumentative

Meticulous in attention to detail: Obnoxious nitpicker

Demonstrates qualities of leadership: Has big shoulder pads and a loud voice

Of great value to the organization: Shows up to work on time

Of course, these are just a few smiles to brighten your day. Every job hunter needs sunny days.

Chapter 20

Ten Tips for Choosing Professional Resume Help

"**I** don't recommend professional resume services. I say it's best to write your own. Interviewers have certain expectations from the resume and if professional resume writers create a false professional image, it can result in an immediate clash with the interviewer's expectations of the person. A barrier rises between the parties because the interviewers feel they have been fooled and the person has wasted their time," wrote a college counselor recently on JobPlace, an internet discussion site for counseling professionals.

Another counselor in the same discussion responded: "Seldom would I recommend that job seekers write their own resumes, regardless of their intelligence or writing ability. They lack objectivity and often spin their wheels trying to focus on the wrong things, either over-reacting or under-reacting to their experiences."

These two opinions differ because effectively packaging yourself on paper is not a naturally acquired ability, but a skill you purposely set out to learn. A decade ago I was lukewarm to the idea of hiring someone to write your resume. But I've come around to a different position on the issue. While I still urge you to organize your own material to prime your mind for job interviews, the riptide of ruthlessness in today's job market makes it imperative that individuals think of new ways to foil unemployment attacks. A good resume pro can help.

Using a Resume Pro

In an age of personalization — personal financial advisers, personal trainers, personal tax preparers, personal lifestyle coaches — why not a personal resume pro? Prime candidates for resume services are first-time resume writers, people with a checkerboard history, and people who haven't thought about resumes in years. Follow these tips to choose a personal resume pro wisely.

Resume firm or clerical service

Many clerical services do a nice job of word processing your resume for a fair price of $50 or more. A clerical service is a good option if that's all you need.

Most people need more, and clerical services are in a different business than professional resume firms. Clerical services sell clerical processes. Resume firms sell specialized knowledge in fluently verbalizing what you want to do and the evidence that proves you can do it.

A resume pro knows a great deal about the business of marketing you to employers, has the latest trends and buzzwords on tap, and coaches you through old potholes in your history. Writing resumes can cause anxiety in some people who, lacking confidence in their writing ability, fear the document lacks quality. Resume pros recognize this form of risk-avoidance and hold your hand through anxious times. That's not surprising.

Resume writing is a kind of poetry — the art of using high-impact words with spitfire sales power — and few of us are poets.

The seeds of your anxiety also promise a stressful harvest because a resume forces you to see yourself as you actually are. You may face yourself for the first time and be dismayed to learn you have not gone as far in life as planned, or you may discover distressing ability gaps. In short, you are faced with the thought: *This is who I am, this is the best I can make of what I've done in my past, and this is the basis on which I must build a future.* To calm such anxiety, you can hire a resume pro who knows how to use words that sell you with a flourish — boosting the confidence you need to move your job search forward.

Signs of reliability

Once you've decided to use a resume professional, how can you find a good one?

1. One of the two best ways to choose a resume pro is following the recommendation of a satisfied customer.

2. The other best way is asking for a referral from a local career center consultant, recruiter, employment agency consultant, outplacement consultant, or copy shop manager. If you're being laid off, inquire within your corporate human resource department. These people often know who is doing the best work.

The fact that a resume firm has been in business for a long time and has done thousands of resumes is no guarantee of competence — but it's a sign that some customers must like what they do and have spread the word. The acceptance of major credit cards is another indicator of stability. Check with the local Better Business Bureau for the number of unresolved complaints; if the number is more than a couple, move on. Merely asking the firm for its interview success rate wastes time — how can the rate be proven?

Free initial consultation

Request a free, brief, get-acquainted meeting. A telephone encounter serves the purpose, but you may prefer a face-to-face session. Speak not to the boss or a sales representative, but to the writer. The same firm can have good and poor writers. Ask the writer what general strategy will be used to deal with your specific problems. If you don't hear a responsible answer, keep looking.

A responsible answer does not imply discussion of the specifics of how your resume will be handled. Much like people shop retail stores to look at the merchandise and then order from a discount catalog, people shop professional resume services to pick writers' brains and then write their own resumes. Resume pros caught on to this move and developed laryngitis. Moreover, it is irresponsible for a resume pro to go into detail about how your resume will be handled until more is known about you. You want to know the general approach — the kinds of strategies discussed in this book.

Another tip-off is the technology issue. Ask prospective resume writers: *Do you know how to prepare a KeyWord resume appropriate for job computer scanning? Do you use the Internet?* Positive responses suggest the professional is on the leading edge of technology and, by inference, on the leading edge of the employment industry.

Dependence on forms

Most resume pros ask you to fill out a lengthy form with details — much as new patients do in a doctor's office. (KickButters can substitute the worksheets in Chapters 7 and 8.) That's a good start, but it's far from enough. Eliminate the firms that don't offer dialogue with the writer. The resume pro should interview you to discover your unique experience and strengths. You and the resume pro are colleagues, sharing a task.

The problems with form dependency is you may merely get back your own language prettied up in a glitzy format. That's not what you want a resume pro to do for you.

The cost issue

Prices vary by locale, but expect to pay between $50 and $400 for a core resume. Never pay by the page — longer isn't better. Find out the rate for branching out from a core resume to create a targeted resume specifically for an individual employer or occupation. Perhaps you'll want to target in several directions, requiring several resumes — can you get a fleet price? What is the charge for minor alterations? What is the charge for an update two years later? What is the cost for extra copies?

Speaking of copies, don't be swayed by an offer of, say, 100 copies for a discount price. Even if it seems like a bargain, you may want to make changes long before your inventory is gone.

Beware of a resume professional who gives lifetime free updating — it's unrealistic to expect quality work when the professional isn't being paid.

Serving alumni is a trend sweeping across the country in college and university career services. Most services offer some form of resume writing assistance free or at a low cost.

Samples

If you make a site visit, ask the resume pro to show you samples of the writer's resumes. Look not only at content, but at production values. Hire a resume pro who has invested in state-of-art technology: a computer and a laser printer. The resume pro doesn't need showy graphics programs or 30 typefaces with 300 fonts. Nor does the resume pro need a high-end copier — copy shops are plentiful. You are judging the quality of content, layout, word processing, paper, and printing.

Taking aim

Target each resume you send out to a specific employer or career field. Do it either by customizing your resume or by using a core resume in tandem with a targeted letter.

Make sure your resume pro understands this concept. You need a resume that has "you" written all over it — *your* theme, *your* focus, and *your* measurable achievements — all matched to a career field you want. Skip over those who sell the same cookie-cutter papers over and over.

Avoid resume pros who offer assembly-line presentations, virtually indistinguishable from thousands of others created by the service. Ignore resume pros who plug your information into a fill-in-the-blanks standard form, garnished with prefab statements. Double ignore those who try to cover the sameness of their work by printing them out on 11" x 17" parchment paper and folding them into a pretentious brief. Employers use these resumes for kindling.

Also, be careful of the pro who caters to you instead of to your target audience. A heavyweight resume pro warned me that some resume services cater to their customers, not their customers' customers — with fancy brochures, excessive color, and whimsical paper.

Your industry and its jargon

Even the most talented resume pros may not understand your industry and its language. Why should a resume pro learn a career field on your nickel? (This issue is especially pertinent in technical fields.) The obvious question is direct — *How many resumes have you written for the construction (or another) industry?*

If the pro is a neophyte in your industry, try bartering instruction in your field for a price break. Or find a resume pro who already knows your field.

About certification

The Professional Association of Resume Writers in St. Petersburg, Florida (800-822-7279) certifies resume professionals. Professional resume writers, after meeting the required criteria of experience and examination, are allowed to use the title, Certified Professional Resume Writer (CPRW) after their names. Certification does not ensure competence, but it is one more indication that the professional is serious about resume writing. The association can refer you to a certified member in your area.

Using Resume Software and Online Help

Just how good is resume-writing computer software? It's very useful *if you remember to think for yourself* and do not assume that because something is on software it must be correct. For instance, a section calling for references should be deleted on your resume. If you prefer to use a skills summary, delete the job objective section.

The software may make it easier for you to find the right words and layout. Most of the programs cost less than $40. Look in software stores and bookstores for programs such as *Tom Jackson's Perfect Resume*, *WinWay Resume*, and *Adams Resumes & Cover Letters*. Yana Parker's *Ready-to-Go Resumes* (Ten Speed Press), a book packaged with disks containing 28 resume templates, is very helpful for people with problems in their work histories. For the sort of people who don't like to start from scratch, go software! You'll have a computer program guiding you all the way.

One last computer tip: Would you like to have free online resume-writing help? Log on to the Web site of the University of California, Los Angeles (http://www.ucla.edu), click on Jobs and use the resume builder by filling out the on-screen form, hit format, and, presto, an instant, computer-friendly resume.

Appreciate the hidden costs of a poor resume: A hack job can cost you good job interviews. When the finished product is in your hands, you should be able to say:

- ✔ This is a KickButt resume — it makes me look great! It looks great!

- ✔ This resume doesn't leave out any skills that are targeted to the jobs I'm after.

- ✔ I like reading my resume; it won't put the RezReader to sleep.

Get Going, Get Kicking

We've nearly come to the end of this book. It's been fun. Perhaps we'll meet again in my other two books, *Cover Letters For Dummies* and *Job Interviews For Dummies.* I hope to see you there.

Until then, this sign is a reminder of what I hope happens to you in a rough-and-tumble job market. . . .

I Read, I Wrote, I Kicked Butt.

From *Resumes For Dummies*

Chapter 21
Your Ten Point (or More) KickButt Resume Checklist

*B*efore going public, rate your resume. Check the box in front of each item only when your resume meets KickButt standards. A point value system is printed below each box. Some items are so important to your success that they're worth 20 points each on the KickButt scale of excellence.

The highest total you can reach is 300 points; this includes 60 points that apply only to electronic resumes — and not everyone will prepare an electronic resume. If your paper resume points total 240, you've written a KickButt winner! If you're distributing your resume electronically, you need a full 300 points for KickButt rank.

Format

☐ Correct format for your situation; for example, reverse chronological when staying in same field or functional when changing fields.
20 pts.

Focus

☐ Overall impression: You appear focused, not desperate to take anything.
10 pts.

☐ Says what you want to do, proves you have qualifications to do it.
10 pts.

☐ Has theme — targeted to specific occupation or career field.
10 pts.

☐ Opens with job objective (job title preferred) or related skills summary; leads from strength — opens with strongest sell statement.
10 pts.

☐ Internet resume: Strong resume title of 50 characters or less (Sales rep/ 12 yrs exp/printing/San Diego) grabs computer search engine attention.
10 pts.

Achievements and Skills

☐ Your skills relate to the skills needed to do the target job or career field; try to match skill for skill; express in powerful, selling words.
10 pts.

☐ For each skill, cite at least one achievement.
10 pts.

☐ For each achievement, measure by numbers, percentages, or dollar amounts; quantify any statement you can.
10 pts.

☐ Speak of results, not just responsibilities.
10 pts.

Length

☐ RezRookies: 1-2 pages; RezAces: 2-3 pages.
10 pts.

Appearance

☐ Electronic versions meet computer needs, including ASCII computer code (plain text).
20 pts.[2]

☐ White or eggshell paper.
10 pts.

☐ Open layout: white space, minimum 1-inch margins best, headings, bullets — RezReader does not have to dig through crowded, unreadable
10 pts. blocks of text.

☐ Familiar, scannable typefaces; no handwritten updates.
10 pts.

☐ Internet resumes: Each line of text no longer than 65 characters.
10 pts.

Contents

☐ Gaps in employment handled with KickButt care, including filling in with unpaid work.
20 pts. [3]

☐ Contains KeyWords (nouns) — especially on electronic resumes.
20 pts.[4]

☐ Contains GoodWords (action verbs) — especially on paper resumes.
10 pts.

☐ Special problems handled with KickButt care.
10 pts.

☐ Features education and training if related to target job.
10 pts.

☐ Groups irrelevant jobs/long-ago jobs/part-time/temporary jobs briefly or eliminates them.
10 pts.

☐ Translates acronyms, technical jargon, or military lingo into English when necessary.

10 pts.

☐ Contains no unnecessary elements — "Resume" at top, no references "references available" statement, no photos, no designs for

10 pts. noncreative career areas.

Proofreading

☐ No typos, no grammar disasters — you/others have read it.

20 pts [5]

Comments

1. 20 points for selecting the most favorable format for your situation.

2. 20 points for conforming to computer technology; resumes that do not conform are dumped in an electronic compost heap. Their fate is worse than rejection — they are never seen by human eyes.

3. 20 points for good gap management. Gaps, a growing problem in today's economy, can be disqualifying when 500 people compete for the same job.

4. 20 points for KeyWords that permit a computer search to retrieve you. Without matching KeyWords, your resume rots in electronic limbo along with non-scannable casualties.

5. 20 points for clean copy. Typos are hot buttons to many employers — two goofs, and you're gone.

Index

IDG BOOKS WORLDWIDE REGISTRATION CARD

RETURN THIS REGISTRATION CARD FOR FREE CATALOG

Title of this book: **Resumes For Dummies™**

My overall rating of this book: ❏ Very good [1]   ❏ Good [2]   ❏ Satisfactory [3]   ❏ Fair [4]   ❏ Poor [5]

How I first heard about this book:

❏ Found in bookstore; name: [6] _____   ❏ Book review: [7] _____

❏ Advertisement: [8] _____   ❏ Catalog: [9] _____

❏ Word of mouth; heard about book from friend, co-worker, etc.: [10] _____   ❏ Other: [11] _____

What I liked most about this book:

_____

_____

What I would change, add, delete, etc., in future editions of this book:

_____

_____

Other comments: _____

Number of computer books I purchase in a year: ❏ 1 [12]   ❏ 2-5 [13]   ❏ 6-10 [14]   ❏ More than 10 [15]

I would characterize my computer skills as: ❏ Beginner [16]   ❏ Intermediate [17]   ❏ Advanced [18]   ❏ Professional [19]

I use ❏ DOS [20]   ❏ Windows [21]   ❏ OS/2 [22]   ❏ Unix [23]   ❏ Macintosh [24]   ❏ Other: [25]_____
(please specify)

I would be interested in new books on the following subjects:
(please check all that apply, and use the spaces provided to identify specific software)

❏ Word processing: [26] _____   ❏ Spreadsheets: [27] _____

❏ Data bases: [28] _____   ❏ Desktop publishing: [29] _____

❏ File Utilities: [30] _____   ❏ Money management: [31] _____

❏ Networking: [32] _____   ❏ Programming languages: [33] _____

❏ Other: [34] _____

I use a PC at (please check all that apply): ❏ home [35]   ❏ work [36]   ❏ school [37]   ❏ other: [38] _____

The disks I prefer to use are ❏ 5.25 [39]   ❏ 3.5 [40]   ❏ other: [41]_____

I have a CD ROM: ❏ yes [42]   ❏ no [43]

I plan to buy or upgrade computer hardware this year: ❏ yes [44]   ❏ no [45]

I plan to buy or upgrade computer software this year: ❏ yes [46]   ❏ no [47]

Name: _____   Business title: [48] _____   Type of Business: [49] _____

Address (❏ home [50] ❏ work [51]/Company name: _____)

Street/Suite# _____

City [52]/State [53]/Zipcode [54]: _____   Country [55] _____

❏ **I liked this book!** You may quote me by name in future
IDG Books Worldwide promotional materials.

My daytime phone number is _____

IDG BOOKS

®

THE WORLD OF
COMPUTER
KNOWLEDGE

Find Out Why Over 25 Million Readers Love the ...For Dummies® Titles from IDG Books!

"Joyce Lain Kennedy is at the top of her field. She provides you with the tools and resources you need to find a job in today's tough job market." — William O. Warren, President, Online Career Center

"If all new college graduates had a Joyce Lain Kennedy to guide them through their job search, there certainly would be fewer unfocused, frazzled, jobless people." — Dr. Drema K. Howard, Director, Career Resource Center, University of South Florida

Filled with Expert Tips for Creating "KickButt" Resumes!

Have you put-off updating your resume because you're not sure where to start? Are you looking for a job change but are too afraid to take those first few steps to get your resume in order? There's no need to stress!

Resumes For Dummies™ is your down-to-earth guide for creating a "KickButt" resume that demands results and lands you a job interview. Starting with the basics, you'll learn how to develop a resume with step-by-step explanations for the resume factors that work for you and against you. Anyone, from a recent graduate to an experienced worker to a victim of downsizing, benefits from the expert tips, techniques, and sample resumes and templates found in this resume guide for the '90s!

Inside, you'll discover how to:

- Determine what kind of resume style works best for you and your employment history
- Use "KeyWords" and catch-phrases throughout your resume for impact
- Nail down the right resume look by choosing the correct paper, the perfect typeface, and the appropriate length
- Present difficult issues like demotion, unemployment, and lack of experience in a positive way

- Benefit from expert advice and strategies to get your resume noticed
- Use electronic and computer resources to search for job openings and other career leads
- Spot the 30 most common resume mistakes

Let These Icons Guide You!

 Highlights features that will make your resume stand out from the crowd

 Signals info and tips that are important for beginners

 Pinpoints advice that gives seasoned veterans a jump start

About the Author

Joyce Lain Kennedy is a nationally syndicated careers columnist appearing in more than 100 newspapers around the country. She's written several cutting-edge career books geared toward taking advantage of the technology available for job hunting today, as well as a comprehensive career guide. She has her own World Wide Web page on the Internet in the Online Career Center and in E-Span. She is the author of IDG Books' *Cover Letters For Dummies™* and *Job Interviews For Dummies.™*

Ask for Other IDG Books ...For Dummies® Titles to Help You Land the Job You Want!

Also look for *Cover Letters For Dummies,™* by Joyce Lain Kennedy, your essential reference for creating "RedHot" cover letters, and *Job Interviews For Dummies,™* the fun and easy way to have a "ShowStopper" interview!

The Fun and Easy Way, the IDG Books Worldwide logos, Dummies Man, ---- For Dummies, and Your First Aid are trademarks, and the ...For Dummies logo, A Reference For the Rest of Us!, and ...For Dummies are registered trademarks under exclusive license to IDG Books Worldwide, Inc., from International Data Group, Inc.

Printed in the U.S.A.

 Dummies Press
a division of
IDG Books Worldwide, Inc.
An International
Data Group Company
see us at:
http://www.dummies.com
for info on other IDG Books titles:
http://www.idgbooks.com

ISBN 1-56884-396-8
5129